BECOMING A
NINJA WARRIOR

A Quest to Recover the Secret Legacy of
Japan's Most Secret Warriors

Martin Faulks

Ian Allan
PUBLISHING

Dedicated to my wife Philippa
who knows much of the
Art of Enduring.

Bcoming a Ninja Warrior
Martin Faulks

First published 2010

ISBN 978 0 7110 3432 7

Published by Ian Allan Publishing

an imprint of Ian Allan Publishing Ltd, Hersham, Surrey KT12 4RG.
Printed in England by Ian Allan Printing Ltd, Hersham, Surrey KT12 4RG.

Visit the Ian Allan Publishing website at www.ianallanpublishing.com
Distributed in the United States of America and Canada by BookMasters
Distribution Services.

Contents

ACKNOWLEDGEMENTS

I would like to thank David Allan from Ian Allan Publishing for always believing in me, and Mark Beynon for his editing prowess and for bringing order to the project.

My sincere gratitude goes to my teachers Richard Roper, Bo ou Mander, Karl Foster, Stephen K. Hayes, Michael Pearce, Noguchi Sensei, Oguri Sensei and Hatsumi Sensei for their tuition and wisdom.

I would also like to thank Julian Chater and Ileen Maisel, as without friends like these I don't know if I could have achieved this goal.

Photos and Illustration Acknowledgements
Thank you to Stephen K. Hayes for the use of the Kamae pictures and to James Norris and Shane Stephens for the To-Shin Do photos. Thank you to Mark Lithgow and Michael Pearce for the pictures from the Bujinkan Hombo dojo.

INTRODUCTION

The word 'Ninja' instantly brings to mind the image of a martial arts master in a black suit, who uses silent cunning and exotic weapons to assassinate his opponents. A master of a secret art that allows him to become invisible, read minds and even control the very forces of nature. This image is so powerful that in the West our entire culture is infiltrated with the Ninja. They appear in our films, songs, cartoons, comic books and novels in a myriad of forms and countless guises. Batman was trained as a Ninja, James Bond has a Ninja arch enemy, but is there more to this legend than black suits, teenage mutant turtles and throwing stars?

'Ninja' is a Japanese word and in the original Japanese script is constructed of two pictograms. *(See fig.1)*

The first figure is of the word *Nin*, 'to do quietly' or 'to do so as not to be perceived by others'. Perhaps this is best summed up by the western words 'stealth' and 'invisibility'. The second figure *Ja* means 'person'.

The art of the Ninja is called Ninjutsu, which is also constructed of two figures. *(See fig.2)*

The *Nin* of Ninjutsu is the same as that in Ninja, whereas *Jutsu* means skill or art, so Ninjutsu means 'the skill of going unperceived' or 'the art of stealth'; hence, Ninja may be translated as 'one skilled in the art of stealth'. But *Nin* can also mean 'to endure'. So one alternative meaning is 'the art of enduring' or 'one who is skilled in the art of enduring'.

The original Ninja recorded in Japanese history were in fact a group of highly trained warriors who lived up to both possible interpretations of their name. They were not only skilled in the invisible arts but also legendary for their ability to live through difficult and dangerous circumstances. The Ninja were a group who chose not to be limited by the strict Samurai warrior code. The Way of Samurai, or Bushido as it was called, consisted of a very rigid code of conduct with a focus on directness, truthfulness and self-discipline. Being free of this code of conduct meant that the Ninja had many strategies open to them which could not be practised by other warriors of the time. They perfected a system of extremely sophisticated warfare that incorporated techniques of assassination, espionage, information gathering and spiritual development. When the odds were against a family or army the Ninja

5

Fig.1   Fig.2

could be hired to bring victory when others could not. The Ninja favoured cunning and subtlety over the Samurai forcefulness and directness, applying the method that required minimum effort to achieve a result while exposing themselves to the least amount of danger. Often a few Ninja could achieve through subtle social manipulation or deception what it would take many years of bloody combat to be achieved through normal means.

In this respect Ninjutsu was simply the art of winning. Because of their freedom from such concepts as honour and fair play Ninjas were infinitely adaptable and thus able to truly focus their creativity on achieving their goals without consideration of others' opinions. But where did this elite fighting force come from and how did they evolve?

The first recorded use of the word 'Ninja' occurred in 1367 in a text called the *Taiheiki* (太平記) which was a chronicle of the Nanbokucho

Wars or the 'wars between the courts'. It states that:

... the fall on the side of the court would benefit the enemies of the northern provinces who remembered the approach through the valley. One night, under the cover of rain and wind Hachiman-yam was approached by the highly skilled Ninja who set fire to the temple.

The same text also tells us of an assassination by a young man called Kumawaka which really demonstrates Ninja cunning.

Young Kumawaka was just 13 years old when his father was sentenced to death. He travelled many miles to see his father on his death bed but the cruel monk who had been put in charge of his father's imprisonment forbade them from meeting to say his last goodbye. Denied from hearing the last words of his father, young Kumawaka took a vow to get revenge. This was quite a challenge as the monk was supported by his powerful family and guards. But in true Ninja tradition even though he was physically weak and without resources, the boy used his cunning and stealth against his enemy and hatched a plan. He pretended he was too ill to return with his father's remains. So convincing was his act that the monk's family took him in and gave him a room to stay.

Each evening while everyone was fast asleep, he collected information about the security of the house and when the guards patrolled.

One night he sneaked into the room of the monk. He knew that the monk slept with a lit lamp in the room. Therefore, clever Kumawaka opened the windows. Attracted by the light of the lamp, some moths flew into the room and soon put out the lamp. In the darkness he stole the monk's sword and stabbed him to death in his sleep.

He ran away and reached the bank of the moat. Then the clever Kumawaka escaped without making a noise by swinging across a slender bamboo tree, which bent from his weight to reach across the river.

This is the first of many Japanese records from the time in which we hear great tales of warriors who use cunning and Ninja-like skills. This and other contemporary stories tell us of a skilled set of warriors with such cunning and skill that it is almost impossible for the modern mind to conceive of them. Many of their methods have all the skill and mystery of a modern magic trick, something that seems not to have existed to this degree in any other time and culture.

Judging by the records, Ninja were most prevalent from about 1460 until 1650 and developed as a counter-culture amongst certain repressed mountain-dwelling families. Ninjutsu seems to have been developed as a form of self-protection against stronger Samurai families with differing political and spiritual views. However, almost all of the historical documentation about Ninja consists of third-party accounts of Ninja activity and legends about Ninja, so it is not easy to see the motives leading to their evolution clearly. But one of the most exciting things that we do discover from reading these texts is that the public's perception of the Ninja has not changed much. Japanese legends from the time tell us of Ninja masters being able to use secret hand signs to channel magical powers, read minds, become invisible and control the forces of nature. Early tradition talks of the Ninja evolving from or being taught by 'Tengu', beaked and winged demons, or 'Kami', Nature spirits that control wind, sunlight or rain. This tells us much about how the world viewed them at the time. But what of the self-identity of the Ninja? Luckily we do have some texts which were actually written by the Ninja themselves! These few records are in fact training or instruction manuals written by the Ninja Masters for their students, all of which date from the 16th century. The best known of these texts is entitled the *Bansenshukai* (万川集海), which translates as 'Sea of Myriad Rivers Merging', but we also have two smaller texts called the *Ninpiden* and the *Shoninki*.

The *Bansenshukai*, being the most complete of the texts, is a collection of Ninja knowledge widely regarded as being a complete culmination of Ninja philosophy, military strategy, astrology and weapons. The first thing that strikes one upon reading the text is that it has been largely influenced by Chinese thought as it quotes large sections from Lao Tzu's *Art of War* and from various Taoist documents of the era. The rest of the text contains chapters that consist of both diagrams of equipment to be used and matters of Ninja philosophy and strategy. From this and other texts it is clear that the Ninja beliefs and practices were strongly influenced by Chinese mysticism and esoteric knowledge from India and Tibet.

The exciting thing we learn from these texts is that the Ninja had roughly the same view of themselves as the general public did. They certainly believed in the development of mystical powers, and the texts do indeed focus on techniques of assassination, illusion, pyrotechnics and stealth, with this important difference: the Ninja firmly believed themselves to be men of morals and virtue, secret heroes who were guarding the balance of, and restoring harmony to, the world. For the Ninja, morality was internal; their actions would be made in line with their vision of totality and so they restored harmony to the world around them. This concept of internal morality or correctness is called *Seishin*.

The *Bansenshukai* warns that a Ninja must have *Seishin* (correct heart and mind) or his techniques of mental manipulation and deception will turn on him.

It is said that not cultivating Seishin *will cause confusion and distress. The meaning of 'correct heart' is the adherence to virtue, righteousness, loyalty and sincerity. Without maintaining virtue, righteousness, loyalty and sincerity, it will be impossible to have intrepid spirit.*

Perhaps then the Ninja were the victims of their own success. As the power-hungry troublemakers were eliminated, Japan became unified under one leader. Through the peaceful rule of the Tokugawa Shoguns the demand for Ninja disappeared. Highly trained assassins became bodyguards, manual workers and many even turned to crime. Although there were a few opportunities for single missions in the next 100 years, the true heyday of the Ninja was over. Historians across the world claim that this was the end of the long Ninja tradition, a tradition that some claim is as old as Japan itself. It is conventionally believed that no historically genuine Ninja school remains in the modern day. But is the idea of there being a genuine remaining school of Ninjutsu so unbelievable?

Ninjutsu is, as mentioned previously, the art of enduring and if any art could have continued undercover for the last 300 years surely an art which is built so completely on the whole concept of enduring through anything is the most likely to do so.

Likewise I feel that those who doubted the continued existence of the art must simply not have understood the nature of the Japanese culture. The Japanese have the most traditional and most disciplined culture on earth. In Japan we have religious and poetic traditions that have been kept unbroken for over 1000 years and traditional dances still performed with the exact steps and movements that date from the exact time of the Ninja. It seems very illogical to believe that a dance could survive where a martial art and philosophy of enduring would not. Olympic sports such as shot-put and Greco-Roman wrestling have survived over 2000 years.

In the 1980s, on the back of the Bruce Lee Kung Fu boom, there was an unprecedented explosion in interest in all things Ninja. The craze was so powerful that it covered the whole of the English-speaking world. Low-quality films featuring Ninja assassins flooded the market, and martial arts suppliers started to stock throwing stars, Ninja hoods and an assortment of exotic weapons.

During this period hundreds of Ninja schools and Ninja authorities appeared, all claiming to be the genuine art but most of them as far from the genuine tradition as their fictional counterparts. In addition to this, of the teachers whose knowledge may seem to come from a genuine source, unfortunately very few modern practitioners embrace the full extent of the art or dedicate themselves sufficiently to its practice. The first real challenge for a student is to tell the real masters from the crowd of pretenders and wannabes.

So perhaps somewhere hidden in the modern world is a genuine Ninja master of an elite team of spiritual warriors preserving the tradition and maintaining their deadly art. If I found the real Ninja, would they have mystical skills they could teach me that would allow me to do supernatural things or would all be tricks and illusion? Is it possible for a man to become so skilled that he could kill with one strike, or are these myths encouraged by the Ninja themselves as a way to scare the gullible?

Is it possible to learn these mystic arts and rediscover the truth?

This book follows my quest to do exactly that. I knew that this quest would be hard but I also knew that if I could succeed, the rewards would be immeasurable. To understand my motivation in taking on this mammoth quest it is important the reader knows that I came to this not as a novice but as an experienced martial artist. Before I donned my first Ninja mask I was already a black belt and a three-time national martial arts champion, having been trained in both Kuk Sool Won (Korean mixed martial arts) and Wushu (Chinese mixed martial arts) from a young age.

It was partly my disappointment with the practical abilities of these martial arts and those I had seen being taught that led me to the Ninja quest. Could it be that many modern martial arts are like paper tigers? They look scary but have no real combat value due to never having been honed in real combat. For example, Taekwondo, which was founded in 1955, and Judo, which began in 1882, are sports. They are designed to look good and function well under artificial rules. Ninjutsu developed at a time when martial arts were studied only if they were effective and conferred benefits on their practitioners when ineffective systems of martial arts died out due to natural selection or the practitioner who could not defend himself died and so did not pass on his ideas about fighting. If Ninjutsu really had survived would it be possible to find the ultimate martial art?

Could Ninjutsu hold the most powerful martial key? Something which has been lost or ignored by modern martial arts? The key to the power of the mind, the most important weapon in combat? I have often noticed that most modern martial artists when confronted by a dangerous situation let fear get the better of them so they respond as anyone else would, forgetting all their training. Could Ninjutsu hold the key to combating this reaction? And are the legends of the Ninja's supernatural and psychic powers based on fact?

The only way for the world to finally know the answer to these and many other questions is if one man was to practise it with his whole being, an honest heart, open mind and tremendous dedication. This book is the story of how for the last five years I have dedicated myself to exactly that. In my quest I have held nothing back and truly given it my all. For these reasons I have travelled across the world to seek instruction from many different teachers and have really had to pressure test everything I have learned. If it is genuine it would work. Nothing has been accepted at its face value; everything has been tested in real-life situations. In this book I present only my training with the schools that I have found to be effective and that I believe to be totally genuine. I give this information with no political motives. I have fully occupied myself with the sole objective of gaining the skills that have made the Ninja legendary.

I have attempted to discover the truth by being the truth. I promise the reader I have not let anything hold me back and have given this quest my all.

However, as the reader will discover, I have found the challenges these arts presented me to be phenomenal and my training continually tested me to my absolute limit. The art of Ninjutsu is not just a martial art or system of physical combat; it is a complete system of whole personal empowerment and spiritual training. It requires the student to undertake intensive training and to rethink not only the way he views the world around him but also the way he views himself and interacts with others. In the chapters that follow I have done my best to recall the tuition I received and to accurately portray the true lessons of Ninjutsu. I want to make clear that I do not view myself as a great authority on the art of Ninjutsu but as a beginner. The responsibility for any mistakes or misinterpretation of the path is my own; any success I have had is due to my teachers.

CHAPTER ONE

FAKES, THIEVES AND JOKERS

G et ready to get out!" Karl gestured to me. The car swerved as he momentarily took his hand off the steering wheel. Shaun grabbed the door handle partly to steady himself and partly in preparation to open it for me. He positioned himself so as to give me a clear jump. A second police siren – this one more distant – joined the first. I looked at the car's speedometer. We were going about 80mph through the back lanes of rural England. Shaun was calling out to Karl, shouting commands like a rally driver's buddy. Just then there was a sudden jolt as if the car had been struck by something. I looked back and realised that the car had just driven straight over the middle of a roundabout. The police car behind didn't follow the same route and paid attention to the normal circular path designated by the road. This gave Karl enough time to take us temporarily out of view. He slowed the car and Shaun pulled the door handle, the momentum of the braking car slamming it wide open.

"Now!" bellowed Karl.

I jumped and performed a perfect *Zenpo Kaiten*, a form of silent Ninja forward roll that allows you to land without hurting yourself. The cold wet tarmac stuck to my clothing as I glided over it. Our car shot off into the distance leaving me alone.

As the roar of the engine faded I could hear the police car about to turn the corner. I walked along the pavement as normally as I could. Outside I appeared perfectly calm; inside my heart was racing. The police car sped past me. As it did so, I made an effort to look at the car in shock as a normal pedestrian would. The worst thing I could do was to ignore it completely. No one ignores a police car screeching round a street corner at 90mph with sirens blaring.

As the police car disappeared from view I recovered my composure and my heartbeat began to slow to its normal pace. I reflected on the path that had led me to this situation. My search for the genuine Ninja path so far had already been a long and winding one.

It started, as with all great journeys, as an emotional shift inside. At the age of twenty-five I was already an experienced martial artist. I had studied both the spiritual and practical sides of martial arts, but something was missing. Something that had been with me since I was a child was unfulfilled. It simply felt like a nagging desire to study the Ninja arts. This desire had always been with me, but over the last two years it had resurfaced more strongly than before. I had tried to ignore it, but with each passing day it just grew more intense.

When I had made my mind up I went to see my martial arts teacher to explain what I wished to do. Bo has been both my martial arts instructor and mentor since I was a boy. Having been brought up in a boarding school for martial arts in China, Bo had mastered many styles of Kung Fu, but with each passing year her interests became increasingly directed to the gentler Taoist Arts of Tai Chi, Meditation and Chi Gong. For me her greatest achievement has always been a mastery of life. Bo truly has always seemed to know how to live a life of complete harmony with the world around her. For this reason, whenever I was unsure about something Bo was the second point of view that helped me to really understand a situation. I was, however, fearful as to how she would react to my intent to study the martial arts of Japan's infamous secret assassins.

I sat in the waiting room of Bo's Acupuncture Clinic. The smell of moxa filled the air. Somebody's treatment was coming to the end. Today I had dressed in a Tai Chi uniform. I hoped that would please Bo and lessen the impact of my strange news. I hoped that she would give me her blessing to go on my quest. In oriental tradition it is a big thing to ask permission from your instructor to seek tuition under another master.

I was so involved in mentally rehearsing my "I want to train as a Ninja" speech that I didn't notice the patient leave.

"Martin."

Bo was calling me in.

As I entered the room Bo was tidying up from the last patient. After a brief introduction I just blurted everything out. I explained to Bo everything I knew about Ninja and why I wanted to train in their arts. My explanation was not very well ordered but it was extensive. I explained to her about the Ninja, where they came from and what they did, what books I had read about them, what weapons they used. Everything – and all of it at a breakneck speed.

My master took a few moments to absorb the information I had given her.

"So you want to train as a Ninja?"

"Yes."

Bo once again paused. We sat together for few moments as if we were both contemplating the prospect of the future in unity. She was so calm over the matter that I too felt calmed.

"I suspect you may need to search many different places to find the true art of Ninjutsu. You will have to travel to different countries and undertake many hardships."

I said nothing. There was another long pause. Eventually the silence was broken.

"Go ahead with my blessing, but be careful your heart does not become corrupted by these skills."

I nodded in agreement.

"But, teacher, how do I protect my heart?"

"These skills are very powerful; to protect your heart you have to make sure you know what your true motives are. Ask yourself what makes you wish to go on this quest."

The question took me by surprise. I had spent so much time trying to gather the courage to tell my master I wished to train as a Ninja that I hadn't really taken the time to work out exactly what my motives were.

For me martial arts had been a lifelong pursuit. At the age of five my mother took me to my first martial arts class. By the time I was 15 years old I had achieved a black belt in Kuk Sool Won, was three times the National Martial Arts Champion and Regional Fencing Champion. Under Bo's guidance I had studied Wushu, Tai Chi, Meditation and the spiritual arts of China. Now at the age of twenty-five why was I wishing to study a completely different martial art? What was it that the Ninja art offered that I hadn't already gained?

In my heart I could feel a desire burning, a nagging desire, but what did I hope to achieve from this art? Where did this yearning come from?

I traced the history of this longing and found its source deep in my childhood. For as long as I could remember I had wanted to be more than just a normal man. As a child, like many boys I had been inspired by super-heroes and mythological figures but, unlike other children, I can also remember always expecting this to happen to me. I was always waiting to be bitten by that radioactive spider! I think that in my heart I had always known it was possible to be more than one is born as, and that inside each and every one of us is an almost limitless potential. Perhaps this is why I have been guided to live a moral life and to feel that I should act whenever I see injustice. Subconsciously I must have identified with my heroes and felt that, like them, it was my duty to uphold what was right.

In my opinion the whole of the martial arts are based on the same dream. The idea of becoming stronger, faster and more skilled, and in an ideal world the martial arts practitioner would also become more disciplined and noble than the normal man. He would be someone who stands for what we all believe in: justice and honour. At that moment I realised exactly what I wanted. Previous martial arts had given me great enjoyment, and the spiritual arts taught by Bo were valuable beyond compare. But inside me˙ was an unfulfilled dream. I was drawn to Ninjutsu because a Ninja embodies this dream in a way that no other figure can. The Ninja, although an ordinary man, frees himself from the normal limitations through his skill and secret knowledge. He can go anywhere and remain invisible and understand things others do not. I realised that my quest to find the true Ninja was a quest to find my true potential, to step past my limitations and with this power protect and help others. Thus started my journey to find the true Ninja art.

The Quest Begins
I began by reading everything on Ninja and Ninjutsu I could gather. My passion grew with each book I read, but there were so many different opinions. Since the 1980s Ninja boom, the western world has been flooded with self-proclaimed Ninja instructors and authorities. The reader can find countless books written by those claiming to be Ninja from the Iga or Koga Mountains, or Chinese Ninja, Korean Ninja, American Ninja, and a myriad of people demonstrating martial arts they claim to be a form of Ninjutsu. I knew I would have to take time to examine all the various schools, their techniques and the claims made by martial artists. I also knew that for me the most important thing was that the art was effective. The best way to test this was to jump in and start trying out techniques. I would find the truth only by doing – not just reading. I knew that practice would reveal the deepest lessons, and vowed from that moment that I would give the training my all and practice every day for at least two hours. But first I needed to find an instructor.

I started my search close to home and found that my local martial arts centre advertised a class called Bujinkan Taijutsu. The leaflet had the Japanese symbol for Ninja on it and explained that the instructor was a Second Dan (level) black belt in the art and that Taijutsu was an armed combat of the Japanese Ninja. So I packed my martial arts uniform and went to the class.

As I entered the martial arts centre there was a buzz in the room; a judo class was just finishing and martial artists of varied disciplines were sitting at the bar and talking. I changed and wrapped my brand-new white belt (the beginning belt in almost all martial arts) and asked the man behind the bar where I should go.

"Oh, you're here for the Bujinkan class? It's in that room over there."

He gestured towards a dojo with a large glass frontage allowing everyone in the bar to see the lessons that took place in it.

"Just go in. Wayne will be there soon; the class starts at seven."

I walked into the room and bowed. It was a large room with a floor covered in red and green matting with a long Thai kickboxing-style punch bag in one corner. I decided to practise my kicks and strikes while I waited.

Being new to this martial arts centre and the only person on display in the windowed dojo, I felt slightly uncomfortable. The white belt felt like a weight around my waist. The last time I wore a white belt I was a child, so as I practised I found myself making a real effort. After all, as everyone from the bar could see me I wanted to demonstrate to the onlookers, real or imaginary, that I was not just a beginner and that I had superior skills than my belt demonstrated. So I started practising, first gently, but before long I was performing the most athletic movements: high kicks, somersaults, flips and cart-wheels. By the time I was finished, I looked at the clock and it was already 7.30pm. As I left the dojo I realised how remarkably tired I was. It had been many years since I had practised such forms of movement, my main focus being on the more gentle art of Tai Chi during the last ten years. My lower back hurt and I realised I had overstretched, kicked too high.

There were now far fewer people in the bar, so I deduced that perhaps one of the classes had started. Behind the bar was a large bald gentleman with a scar running across his head. He was sitting there with a slimmer grey-haired man, watching videos of Chinese martial artists practising.

As I walked up, the barman turned to me.

"Looks like nobody's coming," he said.

My face must have expressed my confusion, as he added, "They don't normally get many people in the class, and sometimes if they know no one will be coming they just cancel it."

This seemed to me like a very laid-back way of running a martial art class. It was certainly not something I was used to. I sat down at the bar and ordered a Diet Coke. The martial arts demonstration I was watching seem to be speeded up. It was a woman dressed in a green bodysuit performing what I was told was 'Snake-style Kung Fu'. Every time she moved there was a sound effect like on a Hollywood-style martial arts film. I made a comment about the silly noises.

"It's just in their culture," piped up the skinny grey-haired man.

"Just like we put music to any moving image, they always naturally put sound effects."

We all laughed. But when they continued to laugh I looked at them, feeling slightly confused.

"I'm sorry, I'm sorry," gestured the barman, as he doubled up, "It's just that ..."

The grey-haired fellow finished his sentence. "... when you were doing your martial arts demonstration in there he was making the sound effects for you."

They continued to laugh, whereas I didn't.

"I'm Kenny and this is Julian," said the barman. "Pleased to meet you."

I politely introduced myself.

"We were wondering what style you normally practise?"

"I'm a black belt in the Korean martial art Kuk Sool Won," I announced, trying to regain some dignity.

"So why are you coming to Bujinkan lessons?" interrupted Julian.

"I want to learn the skills only Ninjutsu teaches; those of stealth, cunning and strategy."

I looked down at my white belt and realised that I was still trying to assert my status on my new potential peer group. On the screen there was a demonstration of a man practising a monkey-style Kung Fu.

"Listen, Martin, can you tell us what exactly the skills you want to gain are?"

"I wish to learn the traditional 18 skills of the Ninja," I replied.

They stopped watching the screen and looked at me.

"Which are?"

It seemed like a test; I wondered if these people could in fact be the Ninja instructors. I took my list out of my pocket and read it to them.

"The 18 traditional skills are:

1. Seishin-teki kyōkō (spiritual refinement)
2. Taijutsu (unarmed combat, using one's body as the only weapon)
3. Kenjutsu (sword fighting)
4. Bōjutsu (stick and staff fighting)
5. Shurikenjutsu (throwing Shuriken)
6. Sōjutsu (spear fighting)
7. Naginatajutsu (naginata fighting)
8. Kusarigamajutsu (kusarigama fighting)
9. Kayakujutsu (pyrotechnics and explosives)
10. Hensōjutsu (disguise and impersonation)
11. Shinobi-iri (stealth and entering methods)
12. Bajutsu (horsemanship)
13. Sui-ren (water training)
14. Bōryaku (tactics)
15. Chōhō (espionage)

16. Intonjutsu (escaping and concealment)
17. Tenmon (meteorology)
18. Chi-mon (geography)

The two men were both impressed and taken aback. They looked at each other and almost in unison simply said, "Karl and Shaun."

Julian turned to me. "Listen, Martin, it seems to me that you're looking to learn something extremely rare. Almost nobody practises these skills at all. The class you came along to today is a martial arts class teaching self-defence, nothing more. You will not find anyone in the class who knows anything else that is not taught."

Kenny joined in, "Martin, you have a black belt in a martial art. Why would you want to learn how to defend yourself? Surely you already can?"

I was crestfallen.

"Have you heard of the 'Norfolk Ninjas' – Karl and Shaun?"

I shook my head. "No."

"OK. Well, these guys are local legends; they sometimes come in here."

"Do they go to the Bujinkan class?"

"Er, no! These are a very different breed of people. Karl and Shaun have both trained in Japan. They're both military guys, Special Forces who practise the stealth arts you're interested in. That's the way I would go if I was you. But be really careful, Martin. Those two are dangerous."

I was advised that if I gave them my telephone number they would contact me the next time the 'Norfolk Ninjas' appeared. I was also told that they were local and that the easiest way to find them was to ask in the pub nearby.

Thus started my search for the Ninja enigmas Karl and Shaun – a quest that would continue for many months to come. The more I searched, the more I found that Karl and Shaun were known throughout the country for their exploits. Frowned on by many but equally respected for their genuine Ninja skills. It seemed that this dynamic duo spent their time in darkness and that their stealthy feats were legendary. Each time I visited a pub I found that if I mentioned their names, someone would know something about them or know someone who knew something about them. If I was lucky I would even get a recommendation as to where they tended to drink, which always seemed to be different. Each time I followed this recommendation the pub would get increasingly rough. Sometimes I even found that they had been banned from some establishments for brawling. Everyone knew of them, but no one seemed to know their surnames or any contact details for them. But I heard stories.

I heard of battered wives being saved. I heard of bar fights and break-ins and amazing Ninja abilities. I was told by witnesses that these men could scale a house with ease and walk completely silently over any surface. One man told me that in his youth he had seen Shaun jump from one moving car in through the window of another car, and that Shaun had knocked him unconscious in a fight in the men's toilets. I heard of how everyone feared them, even the police. I began to wonder if I dared train with these people. The man from the pub introduced me to someone who claimed to know Shaun from his childhood, who supplied me with a pager number. I swallowed my fear and paged the number.

No response came and after three months of searching I was on the verge of giving up. I have always found pubs uncomfortable places to be and the ones I was frequenting were really unpleasant. I just didn't fit in and it was getting really risky visiting such places. I started to wonder if these two white ghosts really existed, or perhaps I had just stumbled on some form of urban legend. I began to look into alternative instructors and was about to move my studies in another direction when fate dealt me a royal flush.

It's a Kind of Magic

"Ladies and gentlemen, the great Geraldini!"

We all clapped as the great Geraldini came onto the stage. It was my second meeting of the Norwich and District Magic Circle. Today Geraldini was demonstrating how to transfer milk magically from one churn to another. I was sitting along with some other new members watching the show.

The next act was a mentalist performance. A short muscular man with a moustache entered the stage. His suit seemed too big for him, but it suited his relaxed manner. He had a red birthmark on the left-hand side of his face, and a childish cheeky grin.

He was amazing. I watched with awe as he performed what I considered to be real magic tricks. He stopped watches with the 'power of the mind', made spoons mysteriously bend, and read the thoughts of others. As the evening continued the acts flowed on. After an hour of performances my head was in a swirl, so many people performing card tricks that they all started to blend into one. I really felt that if anyone else asked me to "pick a card" I was going to hit them, but the mentalist act really stood out.

I was so impressed that I decided to approach the performer later in the evening to introduce myself.

"Nice to meet you mate, I'm Karl."

We talked of conjuring and about matters of sleight of hand and the other acts of the evening. During the whole conversation behind him stood a mysterious giant figure of a man; there was something about the way he stood and his awareness that made him seem like some form of security guard. It was like he was scanning the room for threats.

I asked about the red mark on his face. Was it a scar or a birthmark?

Karl chuckled and replied, "Just can't resist those raspberry lollies, mate!"

I turned to look at the guy shadowing him. "So who's the bodyguard?" I enquired.

"Oh, that's Shaun," said Karl, taking a swig of his beer.

The moment he introduced his friend, the penny dropped.

"Karl and Shaun?!" I ejected the words with a mixture of questioning and triumph.

They looked at me as if I was a bit mad, understandably surprised by my response.

"As in *the* Karl and Shaun? ... Ninja Karl and Shaun?"

After a short pause, Karl responded. He was obviously taken aback.

"Yes, that's us, mate. How do you know us?"

I explained to Karl exactly what path had led me to look for them and about all the stories I had heard. Throughout the conversation Karl nodded, with a big grin on his face. Shaun, however, didn't seem as amused and smiled only when I mentioned that they were both in the Special Forces. They seemed amazed that I had heard so much about them but generally happy that I had sought them out.

I immediately asked if they were teaching and if they ran classes.

Karl shook his head. "No, mate. Classes are crap, mate."

Shaun nodded in agreement with Karl's statement.

"You can't teach disguise or stealth in a class. Avoid all that, mate; it's all about money."

Over the next few weeks I really got to know Karl and Shaun. I discovered that the truth about them was slightly different from what I'd heard. Since childhood Karl and Shaun had been inseparable. In their youth they were completely fixated by Ninjas and at an early age they made their own suits and started playing Ninjas at night. During their teenage years they had an extremely enthusiastic interest in martial arts and both gained black belts in a martial art called Kong Chang. They had then trained in Ninjutsu and reached the point of First Kyu, which is the equivalent of brown belt in most other martial arts. They had even trained with the Ninja Grand Master, Dr Masaaki Hatsumi. Both had indeed joined the military, but it seems only Karl had involved himself in anything to do with the Special Forces. He had originally been in the paratrooper unit which had then been recruited for other purposes. What he was involved in is a mystery to everyone but Karl.

What I learned was that Karl and Shaun were quite unlike me. They had had a working class upbringing and a rough childhood. As adults they were totally amoral. To me they were like tigers or angry bears; cross them in any way and expect to be scared of the dark! To Karl and Shaun there was no right and wrong, merely 'us and them'. They didn't trust the police and viewed them in roughly the same way as many people do gangsters or perhaps as the ancient Ninja viewed the Samurai. Despite all these differences we really got on and I spent as much time as I could with the dynamic duo and found their company really inspiring. They had an amazing energy about them, something addictive, compelling and alive that I had never felt before. They had such power and such self-belief; it was unbelievable what they could do. They were always up to something and were really fun to be with. After a couple of weeks I became impatient and asked when we would first start to train.

Karl just replied with, "You have to visit the 'Bat Cave' first, mate."

The 'Bat Cave'

The duo appeared at my house very late one evening as was their custom. I had learned that the pager number I had been originally given was in fact Karl's and this was the only means of communication they had. Nothing was ever planned. They would simply just appear, normally so late at night I was already asleep. Perhaps this was a way of making sure no one could ever get one up on them. They kept no routine and were completely unpredictable.

"It's time to go to the 'Bat Cave'!" Karl shouted up at me as I opened the window. I got dressed as fast as I could.

As we drove, Karl smoked constantly. Both he and Shaun were dressed in faded back combat trousers but wore on their feet a form of split-toed shoes I had never seen before. After about 20 minutes, I was starting to die of the fumes. Karl must have been smoking newspapers. I asked about the strange-toed shoes.

"Ninja shoes, mate," Karl shouted back at me from the front of the car, "called Tabi boots. We'll pick some out for you at the cave. It's for stealth mate; they're the best for walking silently."

We drove for what seemed like forever, eventually arriving at a house in a distant Norfolk village. I couldn't understand how what looked like a cosy retirement cottage could be referred to as the 'Bat Cave' but thought it best not to ask, so I just followed them to the door, where Karl rang the bell.

A middle-aged woman wearing a night dress opened the door. She was obviously happy to see us and smiled.

Karl took control of the situation.

"Hello, Mum."

All three of us traipsed through the house and went down a set of stairs towards a basement. Karl took two giant padlocks off the door, while Shaun fidgeted impatiently. As I entered the basement I was in total awe. As far as I could make out, that basement contained almost every book ever published on the subject of Ninja and Ninjutsu. It also contained weapons and equipment I had never seen before in my life. Exotic chain weapons, giant blades, guns, tasers, lock picks, night sights and a lot of electronic equipment I didn't recognise. As I viewed the book collection, one of the things that instantly struck me was that there was no distinction between fiction and reality. Every Ninja or martial arts film, be it in its native language or translated into English, was intermingled with instructional videos. Novels and non-fiction had likewise been collected in equal measure. It was like a living shrine to everything Ninja. On the wall were mannequins dressed in military and other official-looking uniforms.

We sat down on a couple of stools and a comfy chair. Karl smoked. It seemed that he spent a lot of time doing this in the 'Bat Cave' as almost everything in there had the scent of tobacco. I was like a child in a sweet shop and immediately began rooting through documents and equipment. It was unbelievable to hold books published on subjects I didn't know anyone was allowed to write about – guides on how to open people's post without them knowing, written in red ink, and an old FBI manual on how to break and enter into houses efficiently. Most of the manuals were marked 'Property of the Ministry of Defence' or stamped with 'DO NOT REMOVE – Private and Confidential'. Mum brought tea and biscuits and Karl moved a giant bladed spear-like weapon so that she could put it down on the table.

Karl then put on a video, *Robert Bussey's American Ninjutsu*, which involved men in combat uniforms negotiating an assault course. In future visits to the 'Bat Cave' I found that this was always the case. There would always be a video running in the background while we discussed our plans and what we would do later that night. The films showing would feature Masaaki Hatsumi, Shoto Tanemura, Richard Van Donk, Doran Navon or Brian McCarthy. They had collected everything possible from every known Ninja instructor. Sometimes this would be a fictional video; sometimes it would be something designed to teach, but both were treated identically. They would just run in the background and then if an interesting or useful technique was spotted it was paused, replayed and tried out. In fact I found that through this approach Karl and Shaun were often quite capable of performing some things which I was pretty sure were performed with the use of wires and special effects in films. I started to believe the stories I had heard of Shaun jumping from one moving car to another.

As I searched through the pile of books and magazines, I asked who he thought was the best author.

"Hatsumi, mate. He and his students are the only real Ninja. They have the original scrolls, and the skills he teaches work. Only him."

"And all the others?" I asked.

"Fakes, thieves and jokers, mate."

I gestured at the wall behind me. "So why do you buy the books and videos by the other people, then?"

"Well, mate," answered Karl, "you can learn lots from these people; after all, a Ninja needs to learn to steal like a thief, impersonate like a fake, and trick people like a joker."

I paused to look at the picture on the wall of Karl and Shaun standing with Hatsumi, the last living Ninja Grand Master. Could this man be the only source of genuine teaching left in the world? Karl's voice suddenly dragged me out of my reverie.

"Anyway, we have brought you here for a reason. We need to get you equipped and show you what you need to continue your studies. First you need to dress like a Ninja…"

Donning the Ninja Mask

I was presented with my very own Ninja suit which consisted of a long scarf-like length of material that I was taught to tie as a mask, a pair of those split-toed Tabi boots and a special pair of trousers that tied close to the body so that they would not catch on anything. Then I was given a jacket filled with inner pockets and a pair of gauntlets that covered the backs of the hands so they didn't show in the dark.

As I donned my new suit, Shaun explained to me that this was just a base 'uniform' with which to work and that, although during most of our operations we would wear this traditional *Shinobi Shozoku* or 'Ninja Suit', over the next few months I would have to learn to adapt what I wore during our training sessions. He explained that our clothing always adapted to where we were, what our mission was and who we were meant to be. I was careful to remember all the principles of clothing as he revealed them. *(See fig.3)*

"We very rarely wear a full mask as that restricts your hearing too much. The traditional Ninja clothing pictured is the most amazing set of garments possible for stealth and should always be your preference, but sometimes you can't just walk through a street with a full Ninja uniform on, so you have to have a set of clothing that serves a similar purpose without attracting as much attention. Military combat trousers and soft footwear is a good compromise. Of course, you may have to wear everyday clothes if part of your mission involves interaction with people or going directly on from another event. If you have to dress normally, it's best to wear sparse, tight clothing. This is because when walking, one's legs and clothes rub together, creating noise. Wearing light clothing also helps prevent the fabric from making any noise. There is also no need to wear jet black. In fact although black Ninja clothing is often seen in films, in ancient times there was actually no jet-black clothing used by the original Ninja because completely black clothing would cause the form to stand out in the light of the moon and allow the Ninja to be clearly visible in the shadows, so a dark navy blue dying method was usually used. Wear dark clothing, but not too dark. Metal items like coins or keys that will jingle and make noise need to be kept in a small tight pocket or in your wallet so they cannot move around. If this can't be done, use tape to hold the items together as this prevents them from moving against each other and making noise.

"As far as shoes go, the harder your footwear, the louder the noise. Traditional Tabi boots, the specialist Ninja footwear, are the most amazing shoes for stealth, but if you are going into an area where you may have to appear like a member of the public the best type of footwear are trainers, plimsoles or leather moccasins. One option is to take your shoes off for moments of stealth. If you have bare feet avoid any slapping noise on the floor by walking on the balls of your feet. Also if your feet are sweaty they may stick to the floor, which makes lots of noise, as every time you lift your foot it makes a stripping sound. Above all it is important to fit in. One way to be truly invisible is to simply dress in the clothing that justifies your presence where you want to be."

After this detailed explanation I knew I had found the real deal – two men who had stopped at nothing to find the real Ninja skills. I was in awe!

Karl then stood up as if to spring into action.

"OK, now we will show you what these pockets are for. Give me your keys."

I took my keys out of my pocket and handed them to him. Was I about to see some Ninja magic?

Karl took my car key off the ring and handed it back to me. "It's time for a swap."

He then started snapping each and every one of my keys in a vice they had attached to a table at the back of the room. I rose to protest.

Shaun intervened. "Don't worry, mate. You don't need them any more. Relax, RELAX!"

Karl had finished mutilating my keys and was holding out a book. "You need this."

I looked at the title, *The Complete Guide To Lock Picking* by 'Eddie the Wire'.

"Now pay attention," said Shaun. "We'll show you how to function without keys. It's the only way to really learn how to open locks at speed."

Skeleton Keys

The first thing I was taught was how to make my own skeleton keys from a set of blanks. These keys work only on old-fashioned locks from a time when single lever wards were used. The idea is that the key is made so as to avoid all possible wards and still open the door. I found through trial, error and lots of minute filing that I could make a set of two keys that opened almost every ward lock in England. The keys pictured are my personal set. Pictured alongside are skeleton keys for handcuffs and padlocks.

Lock Picks

I was then issued with my own set of lock picks from the Majestic Key Company in America. I opened the packet and went through the contents.

It had a number of picks – some for pressing the pins directly and some for raking the pins in one quick motion; some of the picks had a ball shape on the end, some a jagged rake or diamond. It also contained a device which looked like a small harpoon for retrieving broken keys from locks, and a series of 'L'-shaped pieces of metal called tension wrenches. *(See fig.4)*

A Yale lock cut in half was then produced and I was taught how to pick pin locks.

How to Pick a Lock

A pin-and-tumbler lock consists of a rotating cylinder within a case. When it's locked the cylinder is kept in by a row of paired pins. The pins vary in length so that only when the correct key is inserted do they become aligned and the top pins no longer enter the cylinder. When this happens, the cylinder can be turned and the lock will open. *(See fig.5)*

Note in the diagram the sets of paired pins. The top pins enter both the cylinder and the housing around it, thus preventing the cylinder from turning. The springs give some resistance to keep the pins in place.

When the correct key is inserted into the lock the ridges and grooves of the key push up the pins to the correct heights. When the top pins are completely out of the cylinder, this allows the cylinder to turn and the lock to open.

First the tension wrench and a pick is chosen for the task. Every pick has a specialised purpose for a particular lock.

The tension wrench, or torque wrench as some people call it, is used to apply pressure with which to turn the lock cylinder. Professional-grade picks and tension wrenches like the one pictured are best, but you can use a small screwdriver. You need to match the wrench to the size of the lock so that you have ample room to get your picks in.

Place the tension wrench into the lower portion of the keyhole. You need to apply pressure in the direction that the cylinder has to be turned to open the lock. If you have previously used the lock or have seen someone open it with a key you probably already know which way you turn the key to open the lock. If you don't know, apply the torque to the cylinder first clockwise and then anticlockwise. As with all things, sometimes it's a matter of trial and error.

The cylinder will turn about 2mm before it is stopped by the pins. After a while you will be able to feel the difference between a correct turn and an incorrect one. When you get it wrong the stop is very quick and has far less give than if you are turning the lock the correct way. The only exceptions are some padlocks which will open both ways regardless of which way the cylinder is turned.

Apply light torque to the lock using the tension wrench in the correct direction and hold. The required force varies from lock to lock and sometimes from pin to pin. Again trial and error is the answer, so this may require some time.

Now it's time to pick the lock. Insert the pick into the upper part of the keyhole, then use it to systematically press up and feel the individual pins with the tip of the pick. With each press you should be able to push them up and feel a click and slight give as each one springs back down, having pushed the top pin out of the cylinder.

Push each and every pin all the way up. The closer you get to opening the lock, the more give it will have. You may even feel it partly turn! The important thing to remember is that the pin you are pushing on is one of

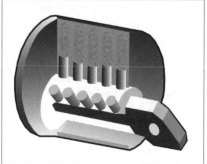

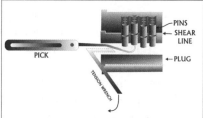

Fig.3

Top: Fig.4   Above: Fig.5

a *pair* of pins. Your pick is in fact pushing against the lower pin that in turn pushes against the upper pin. The goal is to push that upper pin completely out of the cylinder.

You know this is done because, when you stop pushing, the lower pin will fall back down loose into the cylinder. The turn on the cylinder has resulted in a small misalignment of the hole in the cylinder; with the hole in the lock housing this has caused the upper pin to rest on the cylinder without falling back down. Sometimes when this happens you will hear a faint click.

Normally there will be a couple of stubborn pins that don't want to move as you get close to opening the lock. Sometimes you have to 'pulse' the pressure on the tension wrench to do this. You just need to get those last pins to move up until they 'set'. Then the lock will open!

Thief Picks

After I had taken all this in and opened my first couple of locks, Karl had another trick to show me.

"That, mate, is how *they* do it – the method that locksmiths use. This is how *we* do it."

Karl then produced a different kind of lock pick, one that was hand-made from a saw blade. He waved it at me saying, "You have to use the proper methods for really hard locks but if you need to open something fast, this is your way."

He put the pick in a padlock and turned it as if it was a key. While maintaining the tension he moved the pick backwards and forwards. His hand made a kind of up and down motion like someone opening a can with an old-fashioned can-opener. He was using the 'thief pick' as both a tension wrench and a lock pick at the same time, the lock opening in seconds!

The Lock Gun

The next item to be produced looked like a giant robot mosquito. The lock gun or snap gun is for those really hard jobs that both thief picking and conventional lock picking methods wouldn't work on. With the lock gun you still need to use a tension wrench but the lock gun makes the task of opening a lock much simpler.

Used by both locksmiths and police personnel, rather than employing traditional picking or raking techniques, the gun uses Sir Isaac Newton's most famous law of physics to its advantage: 'Each and every action produces an equal and opposite reaction.' The gun opens the lock by striking all of the bottom pins at once and this in turn sends the upper pins flying up into the lock. This creates an opportunity to open the lock which only lasts for a fraction of a second due to the springs forcing the pins back down into the lock. If used properly, a lock gun can be faster than traditional lock picking, but it is noisy and is bulky to carry.

Lever Lock Picks

The next addition was a set of large 'L'-shaped picks and a two-in-one pick for opening lever locks.

Lever locks, as the name suggests, consist of a lock where the levers have to be lifted to the correct height in order for the bolt to be moved. The levers should not be too high or too low. The number of levers in a lock ranges from two on cheap indoor locks to six lever tumblers on high-security locks. *(See fig.6)*

A lever tumbler lock is very secure and very hard to pick. It requires more skill and time than picking pin locks. The time element is a great deterrent to even attempting many locks, as it increases the chance of you being caught in the act. The method of picking a lever tumbler lock is very similar to picking the modern pin cylinder lock, with the exception of the shape of the tools.

To pick a lever tumbler lock you need at least two tools. The first is the tension wrench. These vary in appearance but the most basic and

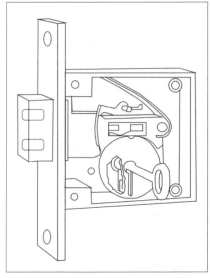

Fig.6

effective tool for both jobs is a simple 'L'-shaped piece of wire. The aim is to use this to apply a gentle pressure to the bolt. The second tool is the pick used to lift the lever tumblers. This again tends to be no more than a bent piece of metal. I was also given some very expensive two-in-one picks but broke those within a week. As with the pins in a cylinder lock, each lever is carefully lifted until its slot catches on the bolt's post.

Owing to natural imperfections in the manufacturing process of the levers, the bolt will contact one before the others. You need to focus on lifting the lever that offers the most resistance. That is the one that will catch on the bolt. Once you lift the lever it will become trapped above the bolt. Then you need to repeat the process with another lever until it is trapped and then another until all the levers are lifted and the bolt is shot.

It is worth noting at this point that if you leave your key in the lock, someone can simply open the door from the other side with a single turn of a pick. Thieves always check the back door for this first. Never leave your key in the door!

Flexi Board

"Have you ever seen those spy films where someone uses a credit card to open a door?" queried Karl with a distinct twinkle in his eye. "Well, this is the real thing."

He held up a sheet of plastic with the words *For Issue to Locksmiths Only* written on it in bold black letters. To open a door you use the ultra tough and flexible plastic sheet to push the bolt back on the cylinder locks. You simply slide it between the door and the lock. Known as 'shimming', it can also be used with small sheets of metal for padlocks. I tried it a few times. It was disturbingly easy.

"How am I going to carry all this with me?" I asked.

"Oh no, mate. You don't. Just carry the 'thief picks'. That will do. You keep the rest in the car for emergencies. You also need a good set of key blanks and a file just in case you need to make some keys."

"But how do I make keys?"

The Art of Key Impressions

A very powerful skill is knowing how to make keys to fit any lock you want to open; that way there is no damage and no sign of forced entry. It's also very quick and low risk as all the preparation work is done away from the site. The best option is to make an impression of the key in some putty if you get to handle the key for a second. You can also take a photo with your phone. However, you don't often get the chance to see the key, or the key is lost.

The procedure for key impression without knowledge of the key is to insert the blank key in the lock. You may want to cover the face of the key with wax or Blu-tack but a skilled practitioner doesn't need this. The key is then moved in the lock and the levers mark the key with small scratches. You then file where the scratches have appeared, repeating this process until a working and operating key in made from the blank. This is a very precise technique and for most locks all that is needed is a file, a blank key and pliers (or similar tool) for holding the blank key.

There are very basic principles to key impressioning for lever locks. The same can also be done for pin locks from the marks made by the pins on the top of the key but this is far more tricky.

Several attempts are often needed before you are successful in making a key that will be able to operate a lock. Sometimes you will over-file a blank and have to start all over again. Don't give up; after a while you will start to develop an instinct for the different types of lock and your estimation skills will get far better. With practice, just a simple glance at a key or one impression in the lock and you can make a key with ease.

The choice of the blank key is also very important as it has to be soft enough to be able to get clear marks on it. Low-quality brass blanks are your best bet. You must also match the keyway of the lock. Once you have succeeded, you have a key that will open the door any time you want.

Finally, Karl put everything in a large black bin bag and handed it to Shaun, who in turn handed the bag to me.

"We'll pick you up next week for your first training session," he said.

I asked if there was anything (other than 'Eddy the Wire') they would like me to read in the meantime.

"This is where your Ninja reading starts," said Karl and he rooted under a pile of Ninja magazines for an old white crumpled softback book.

I took the book and read the title, *Wind in the Willows*. On the cover there was a picture of an anthropomorphised toad in a boat with a rat.

"This must be some joke," I laughed, and looked back at them both.

"No, mate, it's serious. Do read it."

Shaun added, "By the next time we train."

As I left and said goodbye to Karl's mother, I must admit I felt rather disappointed. I had left the greatest Ninja library in existence with a copy of a children's book.

CHAPTER TWO

WIND IN THE WILLOWS

I stood in the middle of the unploughed field. My body shook with the cold but I struggled to keep still; I didn't want to be noticed. I wondered if Karl and Shaun had forgotten me. It was now 1.30 in the morning and we were meant to meet at 12. I had just spent an hour and a half standing in the middle of some setaside farmland frozen to the bone. Then it started to rain…

When it is really dark, the blackness seems to cause the appearance of mist as your eyes struggle for clarity. As I stood there waiting I caught a vision of something out of the corner of my eye, something in the darkness. I struggled to make out what it was. Just a bin bag blowing in the wind, so I redirected my attention to my watch. These Ninja were certainly not going to come.

As I looked back up I had a start. It was not a bin bag blowing in the wind but a dog, a wild dog. And it was running straight at me. My feet slipped as I tried to move but I seemed frozen to the spot!

The animal closed in on me and started to pounce. Instinctively I put my hands up to shield myself and turned my face away defensively. It took me a second to notice that there had been no impact. As I turned back to look, there in front of me stood Karl. He had that sneaky, cheeky grin on his face. " 'Wind in the Willows', mate."

"Bloody hell, you almost scared the life out of me!"

"Yeah, it's a great trick, that one."

I was dumbfounded. I, like Karl, was a member of the Magic Circle, but I couldn't work out how on earth he had done this. My legs felt weak from the fear still coursing through me.

"Let's get back to the car." Karl was already walking away.

As I got into the car Shaun made a kind of mocking scream. Karl joined in. They both smiled as we shot away from the location. I realised that I must have screamed subconsciously when I thought I was about to be attacked by a dog. Obviously, we were having to move as I had unwittingly drawn attention to our location.

As we drove Shaun explained, "Stealth is the basis of all Ninjutsu. It teaches you to understand yourself and others and how to think strategically. From practising it you learn to react to things quickly and to move with agility and speed. Your awareness increases and you gain nerves of steel. Stealth is the foundation of all other Ninja skills."

Karl joined in: "But stealth isn't just about not being seen. It's about making people see other things by anticipating their expectations and their thinking. First you have to realise how deluded we are by our expectations. For example, today when I rolled up to you, in the darkness your mind decided exactly what it was seeing to fit with its expectations. What did you think I was?"

"First a bin bag, then a dog."

In that moment I realised they had been there all along, watching and waiting for the moment when I felt alone and tired enough for my imagination to run away with me.

Karl prodded me to make his point. "Always remember to take the form appropriate to the environment you're in. Use Nature and your surroundings as your allies and then you'll be indestructible."

The car stopped.

"First we need to teach you how to walk. We are going to show you the traditional walking methods. Don't try to be completely silent at first; just copy us. You need to get the hang of using these methods silently and with agility in a variety of environments. As you walk, be calm and patient, breathing quietly and slowly through your nose. Never hold your breath."

SHINOBI ASHI – NINJA WALKING METHODS

Suri Ashi – Normal Walking

One of the most important principles of Ninjutsu is that Nature is our ally. The natural way is always the correct way and we should always make sure our movements are natural and not artificial or stiff. The first method of stealth walking taught to new students is natural walking. The most important principle here is slowing the whole thing down – 90 per cent of stealth is to do with patience. You need to move extremely slowly in order to be silent.

For this type of walking I find it extremely useful to lift the toes and to make a small but more exaggerated heel-toe movement. It helps if you imagine your feet as a curved shape, rolling through from heel to toe in a slight exaggeration. This walking method is almost always better if you are wearing normal shoes. The rubber of the heel makes the point of heel contact softer. This walking method is also very useful if you are in an area where you may have to appear natural if discovered. The best option when discovered in an environment where you shouldn't be is to act as if you should indeed be present. If you're walking silently using normal footwork you will seem less conspicuous when discovered. This method of walking is extremely effective on tarmac or concrete, but should be avoided on gravel or on unfirm ground. If using this method indoors on squeaky floorboards, it is important to find where the floorboard is attached to the supporting beams underneath. Then you can walk along this line silently.

Yoko Ashi – Cross Step

To perform this *Shinobi* step, cross one leg in front or behind the other while walking. It has to be done with balance and stealth. Make sure you always touch down with the toes before the rest of your foot lands. Look back as you make your first step; look forward when making the second step. Cross your arms during the first step then extend them on the second step. This whole routine allows you to walk through the night keeping an awareness of your whole environment. Your hands move around you to make sure you feel any objects that you may not have seen. The whole of this movement should be performed with a slight crouch to keep the body under the line of the horizon. This movement is extremely useful for stealthy walking in almost every environment. You should practise transferring to this method of walking whenever you get close to an area where there are people. You should also practise dropping and freezing at all stages through the side-step. You will find that this step becomes very natural in the dark and that sometimes it's easier to just walk with one arm extended in front of the body than to do the whole arm movement. This walking technique is extremely valuable when walking near a building, fence or other flat surface. Under these circumstances, cross step with your back to the surface. In this way you can blend in with the shapes in the darkness and if you hear a noise or think you may be seen you can freeze by pressing your body up against the wall.

A warning: One important thing to note is that almost every Ninja authority recommends the use of this stepping method for running along walls or thin surfaces. Whatever you do, DON'T! If you walk along a small ledge with your back to a wall and use a cross step, your rear leg will be trapped against the wall and you will either have to step back quickly or fall off the ledge. In this situation you really do have to shuffle along the ledge with both heels against the wall. Likewise if you are running along a fence or wall, don't use this step. Keep your feet straight and run or walk normally. If side-stepping really was the most effective way of running across surfaces, tightrope walkers would practise it as a standard technique. I don't know why Ninja authorities recommend this stepping technique for this purpose, but I have tested it exhaustively and it simply doesn't work under any circumstances. There are far better ways of dealing with such situations. *(See figs.7, 8, 9)*

Nuki Ashi – Sweeping Step
To perform this walking method start from a low crouch, with your whole weight on your front foot and the back foot facing towards your supporting front leg. Your ankles barely brush each other as the moving leg goes forward and outwards in a crescent-shaped motion. As you take a step you should make identical movements with your hands in the air. The moving foot should be touched down extremely gently with the toes, then the outer edge, and then the rest of the foot. The aim is to use this crescent movement to feel for any obstructions in the darkness and then to transfer the weight slowly onto the stepping foot. This process is then repeated with each step. During this motion the Ninja has the appearance of an octopus feeling its way across the ocean floor, the hands moving lightly like tentacles. As with all stealth walking methods, try to keep your knees bent and your body slightly crouched through the whole movement. The deeper the crouch the less visible you are, but the step also becomes more tiring and it's harder to be silent.

This technique of stepping is really useful when walking through woodland or in the dark. In fact it is an extremely versatile walking method which you will find yourself using often. Some authorities recommend this method for walking across wooden planks or a man-made floor. I have never found it very useful for this purpose as the gentle transfer of weight tends to result in the whole stealth operation becoming an extremely dragged out affair and causing squeaking floorboard noises. It is far better to use the 'natural' or 'lightning' step inside a house. *(See figs.10, 11, 12)*

Ko-Ashi – Crane Walk
This step is performed once again with a slight crouch. Lift your rear foot up heel first as though you are stepping over an obstacle, bringing it just above your own waistline, then hover above the surface on which you wish to stand. Keep your toes pointed down. As you place your foot down dig directly into the surface with the ball of your foot, with your toes bent slightly backwards. Continue placing the foot down gradually. The idea of this step is to allow you to walk silently through water, dry leaves or vegetation. This process is repeated with each and every step so

that your foot presses slowly through the obstacle without making a noise before coming to rest below the waterline or the leaves. This stepping method is very effective for getting through dry grass or mud. However, in very thick mud there will be an audible noise when pulling your foot out. I haven't as yet found a way of walking to avoid making noise in this type of mud so I'm reduced to having to use the crawling method if I truly need to cross the area without making any sound at all. *(See fig.13)*

Above left: Fig.7   Above: Fig.8

Left: Fig.9

Fig.10

Fig.11

Fig.12

Fig.13

Kongo Ashi – Lightning Step

The ultimate in Ninja walking techniques is the lightning step. Practising the sweeping step for many years will lead to an ability to lightly dart your steps almost on tiptoes in a quick zigzag motion. The lightning step comes after you have developed an almost intuitional awareness of where to place your feet in the dark. Normally it's best to place your feet on higher ground in going across country or through woods. A skilled Ninja appears as light as a feather as he hops along in an almost supernatural manner when performing the lightning step. As your skill grows, you will find the lightning step naturally evolves out of all your walking methods. It becomes natural and a part of your Ninjutsu evolution. The steps in this walking method are erratic and do not take any set form. It is common to see other forms of stepping appear as part of the lightning step. This step is extremely useful for crossing squeaky floorboards and most hot surfaces. However, don't try to use it in water, muddy ground or on gravel because the speed of the step causes splashing of either water or loose gravel.

Yukkuri Aruku – Crawling

If you need to guarantee absolute silence the most efficient way is to crawl. Whenever you encounter a large stretch of gravel or are approaching a sensitive target, change from the walking method you're using and switch to a crawl. The two traditional Ninja methods of crawling – dog walk and fox walk – are described next.

Inubashiri (Dog Walk)

The dog walk method of crawling is the more effective and versatile of the two. To do this lie on your belly then lift your right arm and left leg simultaneously, taking a 'step' forward with them both. Your weight is taken on your left knee and right elbow as you lift your body from the ground. This process is then repeated on the other side. If you are crawling through mud be careful not to dig in knees or elbows too much. *(See figs.14-15)*

Kitsune-Bashiri (Fox Walk)

The fox walk is the slowest form of movement but also the most silent. This is to be used in high-risk circumstances when you absolutely must not be heard. To perform the walk, simply place your elbows and forearms on the ground in front of you and lift your body up slightly and move it an inch forward. Lower your body and repeat the process. Remember to keep your body as close to the ground as you can between movements.

Dropping and Freezing

After I had familiarised myself with the above movements, we started training outside in the dark every night. I was taught that one of the most important disciplines for stealth is to get into the habit of instantly and silently falling into a crouch and freezing completely whenever you hear a noise or think you may be seen. It is very important to practise doing this for all stepping techniques whether you end up in a cross-legged crouch or perhaps even sitting or lying down. The most important thing is that it is silent and that you freeze completely. If you think you're about to be discovered, our animal instinct to run, move and hide will kick in. Try not to do this, because if you do you will give yourself away. Instead wait, keep still and be at one with your environment. The person who heard a noise or suspected your presence will soon decide that it was 'probably nothing' and you will be free to move again. *(See fig.16)*

Top: Fig.14   Above: Fig.15   *Fig.16*

My training continued like this for many months. All the time I struggled with the lock picking, but need is the mother of success and I soon mastered my front door and the other locks in my house followed. Sometimes it would be very frustrating if I was in a hurry and I had to wait for people to leave the street so I could pick open my own front door without someone calling the police. I had to take this time into account in everything I planned in life, and my front door lock was getting really mashed from the lock picks! I was, however, improving by the day and could open almost any lock with enough time and focus.

When we trained at night, I was always there following Karl and Shaun and learning as we went. If a situation was tricky or they had a mission that involved something outside my skill level I would stay back or even just stay at home. Most of their work seemed to be surveillance, but some very interesting jobs did come up. If there was nothing exciting happening they would create something: normally a challenge or venture that would test us all to our limits. Sometimes these were fun and playful missions but more often than not it was something totally terrifying. On occasions where there were armed guards I would even visibly shake. This happened often as they had a fixation with crossing or infiltrating military bases.

In particular, Karl had an obsession with a certain small airbase. This base, he claimed, was where prototypes of secret military equipment were kept, some of which he had seen during his time in the Special Forces. If everything Karl said was true, the military outpost contained a couple of items that could turn the possessor into a one-man army. Karl was continually drawing up plans and making attempts to enter the base – something I never had the nerve to take part in. I also found a lot of other things we were doing hard to accept. I was so conditioned to respect other people's property that it was difficult to shift to simply sneaking through people's gardens and private property at night. I tried to reassure myself that I was a silent protector rather than a prowler, but deep inside it was hard for me to justify much of what we were doing.

Being at One with Nature

Whenever possible we would be in a natural setting. Woods are the natural home of any Ninja as when you are there you can hide in the dark away from prying eyes and are effectively on the edge of society. Karl and Shaun never asked if I had read the book they gave me, but as I gained in experience I understood more of its meaning. With each night that passed I discovered another side to the duo and to Ninjutsu. In Ninjutsu you aim to be at one with Nature. While we were in the woods, the natural world was our training partner. Often Karl or Shaun would notice a fox, owl or even a deer; then the challenge would be for us to approach the animal without it noticing. It was amazing to see such animals within touching distance. In the darkness of the forest the plants and animals are both your greatest allies and your greatest threat – the two greatest enemies are sleeping birds and thorns. When walking silently you must learn to be far quieter than man normally is – to be so silent that the birds in the trees do not wake up and make a racket. One important thing to learn is that the animals, just like us Ninja, respond when scared with the urge to run, and restrain that urge as long as they can. If you walk past a tree or bush and hear a slight movement, that is the animal responding. After that initial jump they will do their best to stay still instead of taking off and running. If you get to this stage, don't try to pass the tree but just back off and find another route. Another time you should adapt to the situation rather than try to adapt the situation to yourself, as in the case of thorns. If your leg or clothing gets stuck on thorns, slowly back away; don't try to unpick the thorns or push through. Always flow around obstacles; don't break branches or try to push them away; the resulting noise is not worth it.

When climbing trees or cliffs, be aware of where your foot lands; try to place the toes and front padding of the foot in between branches and on crevices of the cliff face. If you are forced to step in the middle of a branch or push up the side of the cliff, do it slowly and proceed with caution. A little force may dislodge a shower of debris or break a twig, making a noise. One way to avoid obstacles as you make your way through woods is to follow a route already used by humans or animals because the ground will be more trampled down and will be less likely to result in any noise. Animal routes are the best to use in order to avoid meeting people, but are harder to spot.

Sometimes when we were out, a person would come into the woods. They were treated just like the foxes or deer and we would sneak up on them. You should match the rhythm of the person you are following. When the person steps with his foot, you step too. This will help mask any noise your feet may make. Remember that sound travels at about 340 metres per second (1,116ft/sec) depending on the temperature and environment, so you might need to adjust your walk accordingly. Note the delay between the actual step and the sound of the step, and try to use the same delay for your steps, only the other way around – you must step slightly before the person you are following.

But most of all use your environment to aid you. Turn Nature into your ally. This is the key to true stealth and Ninjutsu. It was for this reason I was given *Wind in the Willows* as my first reading material. In the story they use the situations they find themselves forced into to defeat their enemies. It's hard to explain but normal people without Ninja training do just the opposite. They tend to walk across gravel when they could go around, they tend to see being outnumbered as a disadvantage when it could be just the opportunity they need. When practising stealth you learn to capitalise on external sources of noise – gusts of wind, other animal movement, passing traffic – to suppress or camouflage any noise you make. Once you get the hang of this you can time a quick burst of lightning step when an ambulance, police car or even just a heavy truck goes by. If a jogger passes, you then have a chance to jog too.

Once you get the mindset of the Ninja the whole world is your ally. The shadows hide you, the birds are your lookouts and darkness is your armour.

Disappearing into the Shadows

I remember one evening during the start of our training when something must have aroused the attention of the locals, as a police car came up to investigate. This was one of only two occasions we ever had a run-in with the police in five years of training. I was still very new to the art so was told to simply freeze and hide. Karl and Shaun explained they would deal with the situation. They went to talk to the police officer and I certainly didn't anticipate what was about to happen.

I watched from my hiding place with a clear view of the drama unfolding. I noticed as the two disappeared into the darkness that they had donned their Ninja masks. The officer was standing near his car. He said something into his radio. Suddenly out of the darkness a Ninja appeared in full uniform, with a sword and in a characteristic posture. I have never in all my years on this earth seen one man so totally scared; he looked as though he had seen a demon! But as soon as the figure appeared, it had gone!

The police officer's legs buckled as he gripped at the top of his walkie-talkie; I think he may have pressed a button or said something. But then he snatched his baton from its holdall. I could see his hands were shaking as the baton was unsteady. At that moment the police car door on the opposite side was pushed open. Then as he turned to see what was happening, the baton was gone! He fell over and the car door slammed shut. In the darkness all I saw was a dark leg in the direct beam of the police car headlights. There was a momentary silence.

The officer and I were both squatting on the ground, waiting to see what would happen next. He was grasping something in his hand. I watched, expecting him to say something, and then the silence was broken. Something was coming over his police radio. Only it was distant and muffled. It was in the police car!

I was startled by the noise of an owl right next to my head. It was Karl. He was able to imitate many birds and animals and often used this call to let me know where he was. I didn't move.

"Come on, mate, before *his* mate gets back and opens the car for him."

Karl was holding a set of keys. I had no idea there was another police officer or where he was, but I knew it was time to get out of the area.

This was the first spectacular demonstration I saw of what the Ninja called Shadow Craft. When you first start to go out in darkness, especially when you are alone, you realise how scared of the dark you truly are. It takes a while to learn to function with minimal sight of what is around you. You also start to learn to be able to see in the dark more effectively. I am still unsure as to whether this change is in the eyes or in the mind. I think perhaps you just get better at recognising things in the darkness. During our nights out we used to practise the art of hiding in shadows. You start to recognise the shadows that are just the right shade for you to blend in with. You begin to learn to become part of the scenery by adding your outline to existing shapes so that people's expectations protect you. To do this when people are around takes guts. In fact guts, patience and nerves of steel are really the most important elements in much of the Ninja stealth skills. Often you have to hide very near the person or even just lie flat on the ground at their feet.

Moving Indoors
As I grew to know Karl and Shaun I found them to be quite unlike anyone else I had ever met. They were spectacularly skilled, resourceful and totally amoral. As far as I could make out they would do anything for money – spy on people, steal anything from or for people, even beat people up. In fact they seemed to have a kind of 'A-Team' role of always helping a battered wife or a dishonoured businessman. Both were ex-military men and this gave them nerves of steel. Almost all of our nights out would have some risk and involve something illegal or dangerous. So I soon learned how to remain silent indoors as well as out. However, I always took great care to ensure that the quest was moral.

It is important when walking through a house with wooden floors to stick close to the wall or find where the floorboards are nailed to the underbeam to minimise the sound of creaking. This principle works wonderfully on staircases too: never step in the middle of the stair.

Whenever you open a door always apply pressure upwards on the handle as this lifts the hinge and helps to avoid squeaks. Sometimes a little forward force works better for some types of doors. Also always remember to turn the handle so that the bolt is fully withdrawn before opening the door. Keep the handle completely pushed down while passing through and closing the door. You also may find it useful to use your hip to push the door against the frame so the bolt makes less noise, and then only when the door is closed should you slowly and quietly release the handle.

If you are sneaking around an office, house or building, always pay attention to how old it is. Just as in the woods, you have to adapt to your environment. In old buildings the walking next to the wall trick tends not to work very well. Due to the longer floor boards used in those days it is better to stay about 1 metre away from the wall. As you walk, be careful where you put your hands. Don't use them to help you balance by touching the handrails on the stairs or the walls etc. You will invariably knock something over and give away your presence. Instead, moving silently, hold your hands out in the positions given in the walking methods; this will allow you to remain stable and balanced. It makes all the difference.

Escape and Evasion

I can remember one day when we were in a wood very close to a city centre. We approached a clearing where a car full of young men was parked on a hill. They were playing loud music and getting drunk. It was normal for us to spy on whoever appeared nearby so we approached calmly as usual. There was an unofficial code that you had to try to get as close as you could without being seen. I noticed something different in the way Karl and Shaun were both moving, something subtle that I could not put my finger on, and when I looked at Shaun he didn't make eye contact.

Karl turned to me and said simply, "Escape and evasion training!"

With that he threw an army issue smoke grenade under the car. Within seconds we were being chased by a gang of angry yobs into the darkness. Karl simply vanished, so I followed Shaun. The men had split into small groups and were running round the trees noisily. Shaun and I settled into the shadows. We watched them with the moon scope as they ran around scaring each other, falling over and even fighting with each other. When they were in groups they would talk and yell loudly like dogs barking to protect their territory; if parted, the grip of terror would soon set in and they would lower their tone to a whimper pleading for help from the others to come and find them.

My training often involved learning to run away from a pursuer. Sometimes it would be Karl and Shaun chasing me, but more often they would find some way to incite a chase. For this reason we used to train in methods of hiding quickly. We would use a gymnastic exercise known as a muscle-up to get up a tree – literally to run up the tree trunk and grab a branch. I was taught how to become at one with existing shapes and shadows so that the pursuer would simple run by, or to roll into the shadows making the minimum of noise. But this was not the only high-octane game in the lives of Karl and Shaun.

Taijutsu

Every now and again we would train in Taijutsu – the Japanese term commonly used to mean unarmed combat but which translates as 'body skill' or 'body art'. Taijutsu with Karl and Shaun meant that we would fight. Fighting was something they both loved to do and in the early years both of them were literally itching for a fight.

Hiken Juroppo – The Sixteen Treasure Fists

The fighting system taught by Karl and Shaun was based on the *Hiken Juroppo*, a set of traditional Ninja striking methods. We used to practise each one of the 'fists' normally with a step lunge, or *Tsuki* as it is called in Japanese. This would involve a big step forward. We did, however, practise from all natural standing positions and even from a squat or lying positions. Taijutsu training with Karl and Shaun was always fun but *always* painful. I never got used to being hit and always came home with bruises, minor injuries and even broken fingers.

Fudo Ken – The Clenched Fist

This is the most popular striking method in the modern western world. This, however, was not true in 16th-century Japan, when wearing hand guards would often prevent this strike being used by the Samurai. So in the time of the Ninja this was a secret Chinese way of striking!

When we trained with this strike the focus was on learning to punch as hard as possible both from natural positions and from more obvious striking stances. Shaun had a punch with the impact like an oncoming train. In fact he is the only person I have ever met who, when trying to break a breeze block, would actually make a hole through the middle leaving the rest of the block intact. We used to use focus mitts and try to punch without any kind of chambering or hint of what was coming and from all the distances possible. For example, I can remember one session when we spent hours getting the hang of launching an explosive flurry of punches from a gesture of surrender. We also used to practise a 'grab and punch' motion and a dodge punch combination. Our focus was always bone-on-bone striking and leading to a knockout as quickly as possible. I saw Karl twice use this in fights, punching with his left hand from the natural position at the side of his body. Both times he achieved a knockout.

Ki Kaku Ken – Head Butt

We used to train doing head butts a lot, but it was not like a traditional head butt. This strike is made using the top of your head, striking directly into the face of your opponent. This movement is shocking, nasty, but allows you to move seamlessly onto the next more devastating attack. This is particularly useful if someone grabs your wrists or you are being restrained. Against a taller opponent you can get really close and crouch slightly, then spring upwards, hitting him on the chin with the top of your head.

Shu Ki Ken – Elbow

I was taught that the Elbow was far more devastating than a punch. We used to practise a lot from many angles, normally with a jump or as a response to a grab from behind or a punch. I was even taught to jump high in the air and bring my whole body weight down on the top of the opponent's head from above. We regularly practised this strike as Karl and Shaun believed that most fights would have only an initial strike or two before moving into this elbowing and kneeing range.

Shuto Ken – Sword Hand

Sword Hand was a complete obsession with us and was delivered like a karate chop but with the fingers slightly bent. We used to practise this one as a surprise attack to the neck from a clenched first. This amazing blow can cause an instant knockout if delivered correctly to the neck and is quite debilitating when struck to nerve points and large muscle bodies. Karl and Shaun were obsessed with Shuto. To them this was the number one Ninja strike. When a Ninja was caught unarmed he used Shuto in the same way as he would a sword; the same strikes and arm movement were employed with devastating effect.

Shi Shin Ken – Single Finger Strike

The most deadly of strikes – all the force focused on the small surface area of the tip of one finger. This strike is primarily used as an attack to the opponent's eyes, but can also be used on a variety of the pressure points. This, I was told, was the first strike to consider if the situation was serious. Not only does it have the maximum range of any hand strike but when aimed at an eye it is the most damaging of strikes.

Shi Tan Ken – Spear Hand
This strike, as the name implies, is used to stab at the opponent's vital points as you would with a spear. It can be used effectively with the palm up or down and even with the hand on the side. We used to practise this strike with force to the neck to cut off the opponent's wind or to pressure points in the armpit or body to cause shocking pain which would weaken his grip when in a grapple.

Sha Ko Ken – Palm Strike/Finger Claw
The heel of the palm is a very effective striking point and does not carry with it the risk of injury that the knuckle punch does. We would practise boxing with this strike against pads or other targets. A painful gripping claw can also be used from this hand position. We used to practise grabbing the muscles of the arms or legs and pulling with force. You can also apply this grip to the opponent's groin or face to stun him, make him submit or to encourage him to let go of a hold. To practise this we would use sand bags. One of us would throw the bag in the air for the others to grab it. This developed arm strength, grip power and reactions. I remember once seeing Karl use this on an attacker in a pub. He simple grabbed the skin on his arm at the triceps and wrenched the man to the ground. A combination of the pulling force and the extreme pain made this surprisingly effective. As the man got back to his feet he backed off saying, "You fight like a girl." Karl retorted, "Fight many girls, do you?" Although the man's words were strong he continued his retreat, holding his bruised arm as he went.

Shi To Ken – Thumb-tip Stab
This Thumb-tip Stab is characteristic of the Ninja fighting method. It is used to drive home strikes between the ribs and can be so painful that the opponent may believe he has been stabbed with a knife. This in turn leads him to panic and change his movement. We used to practise this blow as a blinding strike to the eyes. This should be used as an emergency measure only, as it is likely to cause permanent blindness. It can also be used on the throat or to pressure points on the body.

Kop Po Ken – Thumb Knuckle Fist
Another strike unique to the Ninja style uses the bent thumb in a solid

triangle point that can be applied as a big swinging strike to the neck or the temples of an opponent. This strike is so penetrating and painful that the pain can often cause the opponent to become dizzy or overwhelmed emotionally by the pain. Despite practising this strike regularly, we always found it a hit-or-miss striking technique, although the times we succeeded certainly showed its true potential.

Hap Pa Ken – Open Palm Smack
The open-handed smack is far more powerful than it may first seem. All the force of the strike is focused on the tips of the fingers and can be used to pop the eardrums of an opponent and to break his resolve. The actual noise of the strike adds to the effectiveness and can really unnerve the opponent. You can also use this as a painful method of blocking strikes. I remember once when Shaun caught me with a slap so hard that the blood vessels under my skin burst.

Sok Ki Ken – Knee
The Knee may well be the most powerful strike a human is capable of. It is delivered from the hard bone of the kneecap with all the force of the legs. We used to practise kneeing mainly to the opponent's head in a clinch or as a defence to a grapple and take down. We would knee as hard as we could repeatedly as an instant response in close combat. The Knee can also be used effectively to the body or even to the other opponent's thigh. Like the Elbow, we gave this strike a great deal of our time.

Soku Yaku Ken – Bottom of Foot Kick
This is more of a stomp than a kick and a strike that I saw Karl use on many occasions with amazing results. If you stamp on the inside leg or shin of the opponent the pain and the impact moves all their focus to their leg. This gives you a chance to follow up with something really deadly. Karl and Shaun had both practised this strike so effectively that their kicks were literally faster than the eye could see. They would hit the back of your knee and while you were trying to regain your balance they would deliver a terrible knockout blow with one of the other strikes. To train in this kick we practised standing close to a wall or tree and pushed against it. The aim was to get the power and feeling of a stomp into the kick and be able to strike at as close a range as possible. The resulting strike has a far more shocking force than the conventional strike in other arts. Soon I found I was able to kick from all sorts of angles with great force. This kind of training is rather jarring on the joints so it is best not to practise it every day.

Soku Gyaku Ken – Top of Foot Kick

This kick, which strikes with the top of the foot in an upward motion, is extremely versatile and can be used on a variety of targets. However, we always used to practise low kicks, as the feet after all are far closer to the target and a tree cannot stand without roots. We used to drill hours of lightning-fast kicks to the groin, or to the inside of the opponent's thigh. We would also practise kicking directly with the toes at the opponent's shin.

Shi Kan Ken – Extended Knuckle Fist

Known in some martial arts as the 'Panther Fist', this strike allows you to attack all the areas that you would use a Spear Hand for, but also to hit other targets such as the point on the upper lip, just above the nose or to the solar plexus without risk of injury to your fingers but with the impact of a bone-on-bone strike.

Tai Ken – Full Body as Weapon

I found this strike very hard to perfect. In fact it was really the limit of Karl and Shaun's skill to perform this attack. This attack method literally uses the whole of your body as a weapon. So, for example, you could counter a tackle attempt by literally jumping on the opponent, or you could lower your weight on to an opponent's extended arm or leg. Another example could involve you lowering your body so that a charging opponent impales himself on your shoulder, or dropping to the ground so that a running opponent trips over you.

Ki Ken – Energy Fist

Energy Fist is more a principle than a specific strike. Some people say this strike is performed using your spiritual force. Others say it is about using any body part as a weapon. Examples of this could be making sure that when wrestling an opponent your nose pokes him in the eye or forces him to close his eye and become distracted. It could mean that when you are wrestling you position your hip bone to dig into the opponent's rib cage or for your shin to crush his face. Energy Fist is about forgetting your preconceived ideas of striking and using whatever body part is effective as a weapon. Though I was never specifically taught this strike, I was told that this would come as a natural evolution to mastering the other treasure fists.

The practice of Ninja Taijutsu was quite unlike any art I had taken part in; it was formless and natural. Our practice had no rules, no aesthetic value and was purely focused on finding an effective way of performing the strike. Karl and Shaun explained that the teachings of Ninja were based on finding the correct way of performing a technique for you and your body type.

Although our focus was always on stealth, we spent months drilling our strikes. Once we had worked through the practice of these 'fists' I was taught to combine them into three strike combinations. The first strike was always something stunning, blinding or that knocks the opponent over. The following strikes to a vulnerable opponent are damaging and devastating and aim to finish the fight. If they fail to do so, then the formula is to be repeated to keep the opponent off balance in order to meet with a swift victory.

Tsuigiri

Tsuigiri literally means 'crossroads killing' and is the Japanese term for a very dishonourable practice whereby someone who has received a new weapon or developed a new fighting style or weapon tests its effectiveness by attacking an innocent opponent. For Karl and Shaun this was a very important part of training. Of course, in their view the people were never innocent, as anyone willing to fight with them deserved everything they got. In the early days they would visit pubs and wait for groups of aggressive lads to cause problems, but anyone posturing would be a potential challenge. If a gang of skinheads or bikers was seen, they would immediately get excited. What group of thugs would turn down a fight with two or three men?

I remember one night I had a chance to see Karl's Ninja combat abilities displayed in a rather impressive way. We were outside a nightclub and a fight started. A bouncer had seen his ex-girlfriend with her new man. The bouncer hit him so hard he was knocked unconscious and he had started to kick his victim when he was down. The girlfriend lay on her downed lover to try to prevent him from being attacked. Then to the horror of all assembled, the bouncer began to hit the woman. No one did anything. I think we were all in shock. Karl, however, took action and in one swift motion he stepped on the bouncer's knee from behind. This took him by surprise and dropped him to one knee. In that moment, punching from his left hand from the waist, Karl delivered the most shocking and penetrating punch I have ever seen, which connected directly to the jaw of the bouncer.

He was stunned but not out and as he fell he grabbed Karl's shirt, which ripped. At that moment back-up arrived from inside the nightclub. Two men, tie-less suits, appeared and charged towards the scene, totally misinterpreting the situation; after all, Karl was standing upright, with a ripped shirt, over three injured people. As they charged him, Karl did something truly amazing – he threw what was left of his shirt in the face of one of the oncoming men, then picked up and did the same with one of the high heels of the lady beneath him, which had dislodged itself in the scuffle. In the time it took them to deal with these make-shift missiles Karl was off into the night – a hero with no reward.

Metsubushi

During our next training session Karl promised that he was going to show me some of the secrets that led to his last spectacular victory. The challenge was to touch the face of one of the other men, in the dark, without being detected or heard. It was like a game of 'Ninja tag' and the tension was tremendous. We were in a large wooded area, and Karl, Shaun and I were trying our best to show who was the best stealth expert among the three Ninja. As I walked through the woods, I could feel the adrenaline pumping. My breathing increased in pace and I had to deliberately calm it in order to make sure that I could hear properly.

As I walked through the darkness, I came to a clearing; it must have taken over half an hour or 40 minutes and I hadn't heard anyone, and I'm pretty sure no one had heard me. But then, there it was: a hard flick to the face.

I immediately punched into the darkness to try to catch my attacker but there was nothing there. And then it came again, another flick, this time to the other side of my face. And another! It was like a ghost attacking me in the darkness. I just couldn't find it.

Laughter started to ring out, echoing through the clearing. I knew Karl and Shaun were working together, but I didn't know how they did it and had no idea what was going on. Shaun's voice sounded in the darkness: "Alright, mate, lower your stance, bend your knees. Bend your knees more! Lower your stance!"

I couldn't see anyone. It was a dark moon, and I couldn't see anything without any moonlight.

"Lower your knees." I did. I moved myself into a deep squat, and as I moved below the horizon's light, I could see them lying, perhaps sitting up a bit, in the darkness.

"Flicking stones, mate; we've just been flicking stones. They call it Metsubushi; that's how we were touching you in the dark. Tricky, eh?" Once again, the Ninja had succeeded, through intelligence, through cunning over skill.

Karl explained, "In the heyday of the Ninja if an agent was discovered or outnumbered and faced the possibility of death or possible capture, he needed a way to even the odds, a way to capture a moment that would give him a chance to gain the upper hand and either defeat the opponent or get away. To do this the first thing you need to do with any enemy is remove their sight. It's the quickest way to sow confusion and win. This is why our combat system is based around Metsubushi."

Metsubushi literally translates as 'sight removers'. The best-known traditional form of Metsubushi consists of a blinding powder placed in an egg shell. The contents could vary dramatically from simple ash or sand to ground pepper, nettle hairs, oil or other poisonous liquids. Of course, the modern version of this device is pepper spray Mace, tear gas or marking foam sprays.

We, however, always used a small photographic film case full of powder. Carry them in your left side pocket, then you can pop the lid off with your thumb without taking it out or drawing attention. For training we used flour, but in real life we always carried chilli powder, pepper or salt. All three are devastatingly effective and no one would ever question you carrying them; you can even take these onto a plane.

I was taught that there are five methods of throwing:
1. Forward with the palm up
2. Forward with the palm down
3. Backward with the palm up
4. Backward with the palm down
5. Spraying an area with an arcing motion

Another form of Metsubushi is the world-famous Shuriken or 'throwing stars'. We used to train in both 'star' and 'spike' forms. Shuriken are not used as deadly tools of assassination as portrayed on films, they are in fact forms of distraction. You throw them towards the enemy's face and their natural fear of being blinded makes them close their eyes and cower. If the throwing star causes the opponent an injury this too would be distracting. However, the reason why we practised throwing Shuriken in both forms so intensely is because if you learn to throw them really well, the skill leads on to throwing other objects.

To Karl and Shaun, Metsubushi was about using anything around you. We used to practise for a situation when we might be carrying a cup of coffee of tea. One of us would play the mugger, walking up and pulling out a knife, screaming, "Gimme your wallet!" The other makes an obvious reach for his wallet while using this movement to cover the motion of flipping the lid off his drink. As the wallet is brought out and the attacker looks to the object of his desire, the hot coffee is thrown in his face.

One skill for which Shaun had an amazing ability was to scoop something off the ground, whether a rock or a handful of dirt, to throw at an opponent. We practised throwing anything that happened to be lying about. Perhaps we would pick up some tree bark or some gravel with a roll or cart-wheel. Often we would practise throwing dirt and then scrambling up a tree before disappearing in the confusion.

We also practised with things we would have on our person such as a handful of coins, or a bunch of keys, sunglasses, gloves, hat, coat, a bag of groceries or even a wallet – effectively anything to make the person blink and get distracted.

Another set of items to keep in mind, especially if it is dark, are things that emit bright lights. If you are carrying a camera with a flash, use that. If you are carrying a torch, shine it directly into the person's eyes. It is amazing how long they will not be able to see. The highest level of this skill is in making sure that you position yourself with the sun behind you on a hot summer's day so the opponent can't see you properly. Another method would be reflecting the light from the sun in the opponent's eyes, using your watch or another reflective object.

The important thing to remember, which I really had drilled into me, was that the blinding powder or object is only to distract them. Don't expect it to finish an opponent. This is a mistake many people have made with pepper spray; it is just a chance to get away or to do something devastating to the opponent. Never overestimate the weapon and underestimate the opponent. Never practise just throwing – throw then attack, or throw then run. Drill what you really aim to do. If you are using a spray, be it hair spray or paint or whatever, use the can as a weapon afterwards. Never warn or threaten the person that you are going to spray them or throw something in their eyes. That would be giving them a chance to deal with the situation, to dodge or even grab the weapon from you. In fact you should try to keep the item hidden until it is used. Surprise is the key with this strategy. You don't want them even to have time to blink!

Pick Pocketing

After I had learned how to pick open almost any lock fast enough to make it convenient to get in and out of my house, car or garage, it was time for me to learn another skill. Shaun lent me a copy of a large, rare book called *How to Pick a Pocket or Two*.

Pick pocketing is a completely different art to lock picking. Lock picking is about remaining calm and patient no matter what happens, never getting frustrated and never making any bold movements or being forceful. Pick pocketing, however, is the opposite.

It is about one big, bold movement and about having guts and drive. In films, pick pockets use their dextrous skill to be able to take other people's property from anywhere on their body. They are so delicate in their touch that nothing can detect their movements.

In reality, pick pocketing is about covering up a small movement with a big movement. It's a basic principle used in deception. So a lot of the art of pick pocketing is about how to bump into people.

For training purposes Shaun had a dummy with many different pockets and would place a wallet and keys and things like that in random pockets. The game would be that I would have to enter the 'Bat Cave', see the dummy and, without stopping, pausing or anything else, assess what was in what pocket, walk up to the dummy in one stride, brush against it and attempt to remove the wallet from the appropriate pocket.

This was the basic technique outlined in the book and was something we practised meticulously. Karl was so good that he could remove people's watches as part of his magic act. But, for Sean and me there were more challenges. First of all, it is hard not to knock into a person so hard that their pocket drifts as they fall over. It's also very hard to make that quick identification of where the wallet is, and I think bigger men find it harder to get their hand in and out of the pocket quickly.

The other type of pick pocketing used by thieves tends to be distraction based. One method involves two of you working together, or another where you grab the person at a moment when they are moving from one area to another, perhaps as they enter a lift or pass through a doorway. This means that even if they do detect what has happened, it's very hard for them to follow you.

Pick pocketing was the focus of our training almost every night for two or three months. Sometimes it would be done with stealth, but this was never particularly effective; most of the time we would be drilling.

One of us would approach the other one, wallet in random pocket, and the other one would try to steal from him. Pretty soon, we started to become highly effective. But applying this pick pocketing to real life takes nerves of steel, something that I hadn't yet developed. But little did I know fate had a lesson in store for me.

About this time in my Ninja adventure something shifted. Through this adventure I have come to believe that nothing happens without a reason and that fate truly is the ultimate teacher. The change, as with all great revelations, came from inside and something shifted in Shaun: a stirring, a spiritual awakening or epiphany. He decided the time had come to change his ways. He gathered up his Ninja equipment and distributed it between Karl and myself, packed his bags and left England for the Philippines to seek enlightenment under a master of the oriental spiritual arts. This left Karl and I together, he giving me one-to-one tuition, but the restlessness soon became contagious. Karl started working as a body guard, spending months away at a time in Mexico and I was left alone training nightly in the skills I had been taught.

When you go out at night you often realise how scared of the dark we all are; it is amazing how jumpy you get. It is also amazing how a very brave man can be big, tough and brave in the daylight but very like a child in the darkness. After Shaun left, Karl was rarely available and I started to train nightly on my own. I found I was far more paranoid and scared on my own, the darkness opened up a childlike fear inside me and every noise became a potential danger. I fought through this feeling, making sure that I would spend at least two hours practising stealth in the darkest of night...every night.

I kept up the tradition of testing my skills by entering areas that would test both my nerves and stealth. Karl and Shaun had always made it a weekly discipline to do this, but often the challenges had been so significant that I either stayed home or kept at a distance.

One evening I bit off more than I was capable of. It was a terrible night of wind and rain; bad weather for most people but perfect weather for Ninja. Using the cover of the storm I decided to test my skills to their limit. I donned my Ninja costume and prepared myself to infiltrate the grounds of a mansion owned by one of England's most famous families. I had seen Karl and Shaun do far more impressive things and had taken my time to examine the security and surveillance the grounds offered. I used great patience and stealth and entered the grounds, evading all security guards and cameras, using the weather to my advantage. The wind and rain made the guards lazy and kept them inside. It also covered any mistakes I made. As I moved towards the mansion I saw a member of the family through a giant window. It was such a big window that the light it cast was like a spotlight! The rain began to slow, but I stood transfixed by my success. I decided to move past the window to a better vantage point. I took a step and something happened – I stood on a twig! The light of the room had destroyed my night vision, my success and crucially my focus.

I had made a fatal mistake. The twig itself would not have been a problem; no one hears something as subtle as that from inside a house with background noise. However, a pheasant became disturbed by my activities and flew from a tree, letting out a loud panic call! Unfortunately I was just outside the window in a floodlit position. I could hear the occupant move and fear overcame me. I should have just frozen, but I ran for cover, my feet controlled by terror betraying me. The noise of my footsteps rang out, so I rolled under a thick evergreen. The rain was getting lighter and I lay there with my heart racing. I had never been so scared in my life. My heart pounded and my breathing was out of control. I could hear the noise of the raindrops falling off the trees. And I could hear footsteps, or was it just rain? I struggled to hear over my heart beat. It felt like I was going to have a heart attack. I listened intently. Had they heard me? Suddenly there was a flash of a torch; my worst fears had come true and they were looking for me. One man, then another and another, all bearing torches and all armed. Why didn't I freeze? What was wrong with me? Why was I even here, a grown man risking his life and for what reason? They began to search the grounds. Their search was systematic, professional and thorough.

In my mind's eye I rehearsed every scenario. Should I come out and confess and put my hands up or would they just shoot me? Should I make a break and run for it? Should I plead for my life from my current position? I could imagine myself at the police station, humiliated and distraught. I lay as flat as I could and imagined myself as part of the soil. I said a silent prayer to all who would listen. Perhaps if I could make myself believe that I was not there, they too would not see me.

The torch came closer. They were looking under my tree…

CHAPTER THREE

DARKNESS

Using Fear as your Ally

"So, mate, it's broken you. That's why you've got me back from Mexico. I can see in your eyes. You want to give up."

I nodded.

"You're scared and feel like a failure. How long did you have to wait under the tree before you could go?"

"Four hours."

"Have you been out again since?"

"No."

Karl didn't seem at all fazed by this. "OK, mate. It's time we talked about fear. That's all it is. You see, mate, you don't *understand* fear. You have to learn to use your fear; it's an amazing tool."

"How do you mean?"

"Well, you are viewing fear as something to be avoided. It's not; it's like a red alert, a siren with flashing lights. It's there to give you that edge."

Karl made a gesture like a muscle man posing and then one like a character from a Kung Fu film. "Fear is something inbuilt, something put there to help you do dangerous things. That's why we always train in situations when you could get caught. Your senses come alive and you take care to notice your environment. You have more energy, more drive. The stress chemicals feed your muscles. You *need* fear, you *want* fear. Now let me ask you: did you see what you wanted to?"

"Yes."

"Did you get caught?"

"No."

"OK, so mission accomplished! Now you have to learn to deal with fear. That is your final test."

From that moment on I was out every night. Karl showed me how to sit in the darkness and focus my senses; how to control my breathing and channel the fear into something positive. Karl was to remain in England for another month. During this time he taught me every night with great intensity. I didn't know it then, but this was to be my last month with the benefit of his guidance.

Knowing the Minds of Others

One night Karl said, "It's really important you remember what it's like for everyone else. What it's like to be going about your daily business. Walk with me."

We started to walk.

"What can you hear?"

I listened. "Cars."

"What else?"

"Wind."

"And...?"

"Trees rustling."

"Anything else?"

"Nothing."

"OK, stop walking. Now what can you hear?"

"Nothing new, but I can hear far better now we are still."

"Exactly; you missed out two important things you could hear: the sound of your breath and the fall of your footsteps. With all that noise no one will ever hear you. You are covered by the sound of their breath and other background noises and most of all by their lack of awareness. Most people live in a compete daze. They just do things by routine."

We approached a house on the outskirts of the land we were on.

"Inside that house it's bright and noisy," Karl continued. "Their eyes are not adjusted to the dark and they have never practised looking in the dark. Unless you make one hell of a racket there is no chance they will ever hear you. They expect some noise outside so unless your noise is rhythmic or human there is very little chance they will hear you. When you approach a group of people in a house or sitting around a fire, their eyes can see nothing in the dark. What I am trying to say is, 'always put yourself into the mind of the other person'. You are completely overestimating the ability of others. Half the time you are worrying when there is no chance of anyone hearing you; their senses are all destroyed by television, loud music and spicy food; their emotions overwhelmed by people selling them sex, violence and greed. They have no chance of detecting you. They don't even know themselves.

"You see, people live their lives playing roles. Let me show you how you learn to read people."

Getting to Know People

One of the most important lessons I ever learned from this time in training is how every form of Ninja training should be made into a game. So, for example, we often used to pick a random person in the street and would then examine everything about them in minute detail. We would look at everything about them – the style and price range of the clothes they had chosen, and their hair style. What they choose to wear tells us something about them. It is important to remember everything. How do they walk and interact with people? How do they go about common tasks? What do they eat and how do they eat it? Because even the way someone eats tells you a lot about how they approach life. If they eat with greed and passion, then that's the kind of person you are dealing with. Those who divide their food and meticulously eat with a routine and precision, placing the food on their fork with great attention, are quite different.

We would try and get as much information from looking at them as was possible. If they were wearing a suit we could tell how often they wore it by how comfortable they seemed. Was the top pocket of the suit still sewn shut or had they opened it? How worn were their shoes? Did they have yellow stains on their fingers from smoking? Were there any calluses on their fingers or scars on their skin showing manual work? What build did they have? Were they wearing contact lenses? Even a tan line showing a missing watch can tell you a lot. After a little practice you will soon find that you can discover an amazing amount about people, their background and personality, just from looking at them.

Everyone finds their own ways of doing this. The first thing I do is work out the person's income and the rough social grouping. Normally once you have done this and picked up a little about their habits, you can get the feel for the person and their goals and fears.

The most important thing to pick up is what role they are playing. People often choose roles dictated by the culture around them, and the truth is that people are very unimaginative. Have you ever thought it strange how so many people like to wear the same kinds of clothes and how people who are fans of a type of music dress like other fans of that kind of music? It is very rare to find someone who loves punk rock fashion but listens to Mozart. People are just doing what they are told and conforming to what their peers expect of them.

You simply need to find out what kind of bracket they have put themselves in and then you can build on that.

Once you practise this you realise that we are all actors playing roles. It's almost as if we choose a role we enjoy playing. People do indeed stick to the role the best they can. A police officer is always police officer-ish. If he is not, we really don't like it. So our society brackets people into categories. Once someone is established in a role there is an absent-mindedness about their actions when they are doing their work or the activities that they believe characterise them.

I was taught that this practice is the key not only to understanding your opponent but also to the true art of invisibility. The key to Ninja is learning to change roles, to fit into any situation you need in order to become that role. To do that you should learn to perform the duties without thought and let go of any pretence. If your mission involves being a delivery boy, focus on the delivery. If you need to be a salesman, really try to sell. By studying others you learn the truth about the goals and internal workings of each role or job. Soon you will find that beyond the conscious self there is a true will.

We all appear to be guided by an unknown goal, something inside us, something we really want. People seem unaware of this, but if you look at their life from a distance you can see that this path guides them even if they try to move in an opposite direction. This could be towards motherhood, being successful, or being a victim. Almost everyone puts themselves exactly where they want to be.

Doing the Bins
A great deal of Ninja training is about how to get information on people. Knowledge is power, and I was taught that one of the easiest ways to achieve this was to collect their bins. In Britain it is not illegal to *look* in people's bins, but you really should be aware that taking away other people's rubbish is illegal. However, searching through someone's bin tells you more about the person than you could ever imagine.

You can see if they have got a girlfriend, and if they are active sexually. You can find out what they eat. You can discover what medication they are on and thus the illnesses they have. You can get to judge the class of the person they are: what they wear, what they think, what they read.

The bins contain clues to the essence of the person, the trail they leave behind. And occasionally, going through someone's bins tells you a lot more about a situation and whether the person is an enemy or not.

Not many people use shredders, and nowadays there's a convenient extra bin for recycling, which is where people put all their paperwork, providing an audit of their lives – how much they are earning and spending, what debts they have, who they are corresponding with. You can really get to know a person.

Armed with such information you can go ahead and do extra research. There are certain disks and data sources that can be purchased. The one we always used was the UK Info Disk, which is a cross-reference directory showing the person's telephone number next to their electoral registration information and their address. By combining all of this information, you get to learn a lot more about the person. It is also worth going to the local library and doing a microfiche or database search on the local newspapers, because deaths, births, marriages, or indeed anything that has gone wrong in the person's life, are likely to be in there somewhere, including their successes and information about their family.

You can then take this one step further. There are clipping services that you can subscribe to that tell you when anyone is mentioned. If they own a business, you can obtain information about it through Companies House, which has the database of all British businesses that have to register their business activities and audits.

But most of all, like our analysis of the person game, learning about someone's life is about getting into their mindset: learning who they are and putting yourself into their position, understanding their motives, their dreams, their weaknesses. And I was about to learn a lot more about how to do this.

Spy Technology

The time had come, I was told, to add to my very basic arsenal of equipment. Karl explained that he and Shaun had trained me without such devices so that my skills would develop properly, but now it was time to give myself an unfair advantage. It was time to go back to the 'Bat Cave' and start a new discipline – the love of spy technology!

In their day the Ninja used the most up-to-date gadgets available. We have both historical records and extant examples of a multitude of equipment including hang-gliders, caltrops, folding bamboo ladders, grappling hooks, and items for lock breaking and prising open planking. They had bell-shaped objects for listening through walls, and even special devices to allow the Ninja to walk on water!

Karl and Shaun used some of these ancient devices and many modern equivalents of all these and more.

Night Sights

The fall of the red giant that was the Soviet Union allowed the market to be flooded with amazing equipment originally designed for use by the Russian Secret Service. This is where most of the equipment used by my teachers seemed to have come from, although they would always be on the lookout for more up-to-date and superior models. As far as night sights were concerned we always used 'moonscopes', which were a pair of binoculars that amplified the natural light. They had infra-red scopes, but we found these hard to see detail with. The infra-red was only good for finding people who were already hiding. Karl and Shaun also had their cars fitted out with a device that, when pulled from the roof of the car, allowed them to see the view in front of the car in full detail in the darkest night. (They always called this a gyroscope, but I am sure they were thinking of some other device.) This way you could sit in the car and watch, or even drive the car through the dark.

After I gained a moonscope a whole new world of possibilities opened up to me when practising stealth. It gave me a great advantage and I would often take time to zoom in and view the route I was about to walk, using the night vision as an aid to identifying possible areas that may make noise or obstacles that I may not otherwise have noticed in the dark. It also gave me a quick way to see in the dark if my eyes had not adjusted or if my night vision had been knocked out by headlights or other bright lights.

The Parabolic Ear

One device that improved things significantly was the 'parabolic ear'. We had amazing fun with this device, shaped like a satellite dish with a handle, with which you can hear conversations at great distances. We also had a laser version that would pick up the vibrations on a window and turn them back to sound. It was truly amazing to be able to hear any conversation in a house, car or garden at a distance. It gave you far more options with any mission because it also allowed you to discover exactly what people really think of you and your actions.

Spike Mikes

A spike mike is used for listening to activities in an adjoining house. Although it gives high-quality results, it is of limited use as you need to be able to gain access to the next-door property. The spike is hammered into the wall as you would a nail and the vibrations that transfer along the spike are amplified and either transmitted or recorded.

Contact Microphone Transmitters

In the days before digitisation, tapping phones was easy. Nowadays it is better to go to the location and use a contact microphone or install a bug. I love contact microphones like a judoka loves throws. They are truly amazing. When Karl gave me my first set I started to place them on the windows or window sills of people I wanted to know more about. Once in place these 'tiddly winks of doom' transmit the vibrations they pick up directly to your receiver. You just have to be aware that their battery lives vary and that you may have to go back to replace them. They are very useful for business. Just place one in the room where all the decisions are made and you can save a lot of time doing background searches or data mining. Just remember that the eavesdropper never hears good of himself. Go in with the awareness that only your mother truly loves you. Don't be surprised by anything you hear!

Mobile Bugs
A very effective if expensive option is the mobile phone bug. You simply put it in the room you want to listen in on and dial in or set the bug to dial out to a recorder whenever a noise is made. Because these bugs are very expensive, unless you can retrieve them or wire them permanently into a power source they are best used sparingly.

Disguise
For years Karl and Shaun had struggled with special effects. They had made many attempts at mask production. However, as time went on they realised that this skill would take a lifetime to perfect, so they decided to seek out a range of professionally made masks that would allow us, with care, to become someone else. The results were amazing, as the accompanying photos testify. The masks truly were up to 'Mission Impossible' and even allowed you to speak without detection. The only risk came if you were very close to someone and they touched you, or if you were too physical and the mask moved slightly. It was a very strange but also freeing experience to be able to walk down the street as someone else and to meet your friends and family without them recognising you. There is something about this form of experience that allows you to discover a flexibility inside that nothing else can. You start to realise that you can in fact be anyone you wish to be.

Smoke and Fire
Karl wanted to give me more options in case I got stuck in a corner or needed a distraction. He tended to use smoke grenades, but these are not the only form of fire used. I was taught to make a variety of fire devices, including smoke bombs that would go off when thrown to the ground and small 'fire packets' the size of a thumb that would go up in flames 30 seconds after being squeezed. These may seem very modern, but fire was one skill that original *Iga* Ninja excelled in. Fire devices were used to cause distraction and invoke terror. Many Ninja texts talk about setting fires, so it seems to have been a very important part of their duties. We, however, only used smoke or fire as a last resort. For this we had two types of smoke bomb. The first consisted of an impact grenade.

Impact Grenades

An impact grenade can be constructed by sawing a few nails into short pieces about a centimetre long. Each one of these should then be covered with paper gun caps and flash paper (a type of highly flammable paper used by magicians). Wrap these together in one big sheet of paper and place on a piece of kitchen foil. Then fill the foil with a small lining of smoke powder and fold everything up into a ball. When thrown at the floor the metal will hit together causing the caps to go off, which will then set the flash paper on fire, creating a big plume of smoke which you can use to get away. Always run off at an angle, preferably past the pursuer, for he will assume that you are continuing your normal path. This device also works with flash powder for blinding or gunpowder for setting something on fire.

Another version is made using a drawstring trigger. Basically you fill an everyday party popper with smoke powder. Sometimes we used to put a bit of flash powder or flash paper near the popping mechanism just to make sure, but this is not really needed. Don't ever fill this one with flash powder or gunpowder. We did this once and ended up with second degree burns to the hand! This 'smoke bomb' provides a barrier between you and the person chasing you. Few people run through it after you. In the moment that you throw the bomb you can use the distraction to get away. With the impact grenade you simply throw the bomb to the ground near your pursuer's feet or in his line of sight. With the party popper version you can have them tied to your belt by the string and they will be triggered by pulling and throwing them. The impact grenades are always the better option, in my opinion.

Caltrops

To impede pursuers historical Ninja carried caltrops or *tetsu bishi*. These were shaped like a tetrahedron so that one prong was always pointing upwards. As the Samurai wore very light footwear these spikes could easily penetrate their soles. An alternative to the *tetsu bishi* existed in the form of the dried seed pod of the water chestnut. This natural caltrop dried into a shape with a number of sharp prongs. Most of these natural caltrops are useless, but we used metal caltrops in a variety of forms: large spikes to stop cars and smaller ones for people. We would also practise with improvised caltrops. For example, taking a light bulb and smashing it in your coat and then sprinkling the broken glass on the floor works very well; broken bottles less so, but anything sticky or smelly tends to slow people. However, if you are being pursued you need to have the proper caltrops to sprinkle behind you.

Cat Claws

Another Ninja set of tools are the Ninja 'cat claws' or *Shinobi Shuko* as they are called in Japanese. I can remember the first time I ever saw them used. We were standing at the bottom of a very tall branchless tree when Shaun took out a set of these impressive-looking weapons. First he produced a pair of foot spikes and tied them using two straps made of seatbelt material in an elaborate formation onto the soles of his Tabi boots. He then donned two sets of steel claws on his palms; the claws were bent backwards like those of a tiger and looked vicious!

Shaun launched himself at the tree with ferocity and using great strength he climbed up, moving like a big black bear stabbing each set of claws in one by one.

I looked on in awe. Karl handed me a set which I donned as he started to climb a very similar tree. Karl's climbing method was different; it was slower and involved stabbing the foot spikes in both at the same time and using the hand claws to grip the tree. He would then alternate the movement with a jump of the feet then a double arm claw.

I started to tackle my own tree, but my claws seemed to be defective. Everything went wrong. The foot claws kept coming off and slipping and I couldn't get a grip. If I did make some progress I would soon slip and fall, scratching myself on the bark as I fell.

Karl and Shaun sniggered from their trees like two monkeys. This was the start of my cat claw training. It took me two weeks to get the hang of climbing with them and even then I found they were only of real use for the kind of trees we were working on that day. If the tree had branches, I could normally get up it faster and with more stealth without the claws.

I was also taught how to fight with the claws. Shaun explained that in the past they were used to assassinate people. If you clawed someone to death on a mountain range, people would surmise that the victim had simply been killed by a mountain lion.

I always remembered this principle. The true Ninja always makes it look like his actions are caused by his own bad judgement, bad luck or by the actions of another enemy.

Newspaper Test

Karl led me into a separate room.

"It's time for your final test, mate," he said. "Let's see if you've got it."

The whole room was aflood, the floor covered in damp newspapers. What he had done was unfold the newspapers, put the spread of the pages across the floor to cover the entire room and then soak the whole thing.

"I want you to step across the room without ripping the paper."

65

It was like a scene from a Kung Fu movie. I looked at the soggy paper and decided that the type of step that I was going to use would be very directly up and down. So I used a non-rolling normal step with a slight crouch to make sure that I did not slip, rip or tear. I walked across the paper, making sure that I lowered my foot directly onto the floor and lifting it vertically without any form of slipping or sliding. Karl seemed extremely impressed.

"Right, now I want you to walk back towards me using cross step."

So I used the cross step but once again making sure the step was vertical and that there was no slipping, sliding or anything that would tear the paper. When I got to the other side Karl was beaming. I had never seen him so happy.

"You're ready, mate; you are absolutely ready; you can do it now. That was amazing!"

I looked at the paper, which had not been torn. Could it really have been that hard? Surely anyone could walk across the paper without making it rip. I said, "Karl, that was quite easy. Can't most people do that?"

"No, mate," he replied. "No, it's really wet and soggy. Let me show you."

He took a pen from his pocket and slowly brushed the blunt end across the paper. A large rip appeared with ease. With disbelief, I bent down and touched the paper. As I lifted my hand back, I saw that every single finger had pierced the paper. Karl was correct; my stealth skills were ready!

An Inner Transformation

My evening practice sessions became the main focus of my day. I started to regain my confidence and my skills improved nightly. By day I would work hard; in the evening I would silently patrol the streets invisible to everyone. By now it was easy to walk through other people's gardens and observe their daily life.

As time went on, I began to feel separate from the outside world. Every night I saw one thing repeated again and again. Everyone spent the whole of their spare time watching television. As I went from house to house, no one was ever doing anything else: no talking to each other, playing music, making love, arguing. No one was living! Something started to change inside. I no longer felt part of the system. We tend to have set views on things like ownership and authority. All that left me. No one owned anything any more than the moles and birds did. The police, security guards, the government were just people trying to make me do what they wanted. The whole world around me was full of tribes. Political parties, football supporters – all were part of a tribal pack system that I no longer felt any connection with. Groups of loud drunken men were the same as a pack of barking dogs to me.

My senses gradually improved and my reactions got quicker from being alert and paying attention to my surroundings for so long every day. I began to feel more at one with the foxes and owls. I can't quite describe it, but when you are in the dark this much, some of the darkness stays with you afterwards. After four months of this training something clicked. I felt different inside. I felt at home in the dark and I started to have some amazing successes. I found that if a fox was in the area I could smell it and if the wind was in the right direction I could, using my stealth skills, get very close to it. With deer, I could even touch them before they knew I was there.

A series of events made me realise that I had changed inside. The first of these events involved a flood in my home. My house was in darkness. The flood had caused the electricity to blow. My lovely wife informed me the plumber needed to be called, but the torch was in the loft and the phone in the bedroom. The neighbours were assembled helpfully outside my front door. I ran up the stairs, pulled down the ladder to the loft, climbed up and got the torch, went to the bedroom to get the phone and then returned to the front door.

The assembled neighbours and family were in total awe. What I had done effortlessly and with no second thought was a miracle to them. How could someone have done that at such speed in the pitch dark without even thinking to turn the torch on? The darkness had become my friend.

One other example of this harmony with the darkness occurred when I was at a friend's house and there was a sound that we suspected was someone breaking in. We both instantly jumped into action, he running around the house turning lights on and I running around the house turning them off. For me the darkness was where I was comfortable and my instinct was to give myself an advantage by putting the house in darkness. For him the light was safe and he wanted to see or scare away the potential burglar.

I continued my process of practising stealth and other Ninja skills in everyday life. However, I found that as this improved it started to become counterproductive.

One evening I returned from a Masonic lodge meeting to my sleeping family. I made sure I got into the house with total silence. I turned off the car engine and let the car glide to a stop so there was no approaching car noise. I opened and closed the car door with silence and patience and used slow natural steps to the front door. I then unlocked it with stealth, lifting the door on its hinges so it made no noise and opening it with total silence. I entered the house, locking and closing the door quietly behind me. I didn't turn on the lights but silently made my preparations for bed. Sneaking into the bedroom quietly, I sat down on the bed and got in stealthily. When my wife had stopped screaming we came to an agreement that although it was nice to be quiet, there are times when total Ninja stealth is not very useful and can cause some nasty surprises! No one wants a husband magically appearing in bed beside them at night with no warning whatsoever.

You're Not Alone!
Of course, I was not always the only person sneaking though the night; there were often others around, depending on where I was training. Sometimes there would be lovers, sometimes dog walkers, hunters or people walking with friends, and often very late at night. The later it gets, the more likely it is that the people you run into are burglars, muggers or, on one occasion, even devil worshippers! Karl and Shaun really looked down on such types and, once successfully identified, they were subjected to all sorts of bullying and fear tactics. Such encounters were rare but I had a few and my approach to them was different. Sometimes I would simply call the police. However, the risk with that is being caught yourself, as if you were the person you are reporting. More often than not it is best just to be there and watch. If a crime is being committed, you must follow the person to his car or home and then report it. If the person is checking out somewhere, warn the property owner. All of this should be done anonymously.

I started to try and be more and more ambitious and found that I could do amazing things. I could simply walk behind security guards in time with their steps. If they turned I would vanish into the shadows. I could move from roof top to roof top with ease. I had the hang of it all. I felt an indescribable sense of power. I felt indestructible.

Despite all this achievement, I still felt a sense of emptiness inside. Something was missing. I explained in a letter to Karl what I was feeling.

"I want to learn the spiritual arts of Ninjutsu. My training under you and Shaun has made me feel close to something. It's like when you have a word on the tip of your tongue that you cannot call to mind. It's in the darkness when I am out every evening, but I can't quite touch it. My whole being longs for it. I really feel that is what is calling me. It seems like these arts are the foundation of the building not the peak or decoration. Can you please direct me?"

Karl's reply took a month to arrive from Mexico. I opened the envelope. Inside was a small slip of paper. It simply read: "Stephen K. Hayes."

CHAPTER FOUR

MASTER OF THE
FOUR ELEMENTS

"Mountain Dew, please."

I made sure I picked the drink I had never seen in England. As the air steward handed me the can I reflected on my quest. Many stories are told about students of the martial arts who go on great pilgrimages to find the true secrets of their art. Normally these travels are to distant mountains like the one depicted on the can I was holding. I, however, was flying to America to spend a month under the tuition of the great Ninja master, Stephen K. Hayes. I was heading for Dayton, Ohio, of all places – famous for one thing: the place where the first plane was ever flown.

Having received Karl's missive, I had looked up Stephen K. Hayes and discovered that he possessed amazing martial arts credentials. A *Black Belt* magazine hall of fame member, Hayes appears to be one of the few genuine authorities to have come out of the '80s Ninja boom. Indeed some credit his return from Japan to America as triggering the phenomenon. Having trained for over a decade in Japan with the last Ninja Grand Master Masaaki Hatsumi, Stephen went on to become the personal bodyguard to the Dalai Lama. This seems to have been the natural result of Master Hayes' personal spiritual quest that had led him to search the globe for tuition from the greatest spiritual masters.

Having found the webpage of Stephen's martial arts school, I was interested to discover that he called his Ninja art 'To-Shin Do'. The meanings of the Japanese words are as follows:

TO – the sword

SHIN – the focused spirit of intention

DO – the path to mastery.

So the whole meaning was 'the way of the sword heart' or 'the sword spirit way'. This I instantly recognised as a code. The Japanese symbol for *Nin* is formed of a depiction of a sword over a heart.

I was truly inspired and vowed that I would be the greatest student Stephen K. Hayes would ever have. I started training as hard as I could and made great preparations. I would attend his martial arts school and take part in every class. I would listen to everything, observe everything and in the time I was there would gain the grounding in the spiritual arts of the Ninja that would build the foundation of my future practice. But how could I do this in just one month? I decided I would rush in with fire, enthusiasm and energy. I would throw myself into the situation with every ounce of my being and hold nothing back.

As I landed in Dayton I was a bundle of fear, excitement and ambition. I had never travelled alone before and was new to America. Would the English Ninja sink or swim in the 'Land of the Free'? Would my plane take off in Dayton, Ohio?

The Dayton Quest Hombu Dojo

I knew that the Quest dojo opened at 10.30, but my nerves woke me up so early that I was there an hour before classes began. This was good. I hoped this would show that I was serious. There is a saying that everything is bigger in America and I found this to be true. The roads are bigger, the rooms in the hotels are the size of European living rooms and the portions you get for your meals are monstrous. I had fallen in love with America from the very first meal I ate!

This extra space allows Americans to do things properly and I stood in absolute awe outside the Quest dojo. I could see through the glass the large, fully equipped dojo with mirrored walls, life-size dummies, body pads, focus mitts and practice weapons of every variety. As I gazed through the window a car pulled up. It was not Hayes. Master Hayes is a big man who sports a trademark beard. This man was small, thin and wiry; his body carried no fat at all. His build reminded me of the practitioners of Brazilian Jujitsu I knew. It was interesting to note the contrast in build to the heavily muscled Karl and Shaun.

"You must be Martin. Pleased to meet you. I'm James Norris. Anshu Hayes will be heading in to meet you later."

He opened the dojo door and we went in. The dojo itself was quite unlike anything I had ever seen before. On the wall there was a shrine with candles, a rope and mirror. The whole place was spotlessly clean and fresh, and there was a counter where books, uniforms and training equipment were supplied. Off the room was an office for staff to run the whole business, and a separate room for meditation and spiritual practice. It was truly amazing; my excitement bubbled forth in a multitude of questions. At the time it seemed perfectly natural, but in hindsight Master Norris was probably a bit overwhelmed by the lack of normal introductions and such an intense launch into things.

I first asked about the mysterious shrine.

Kamiza Dojo Spirit Focal Point

The Japanese word 'Kamiza' translates as 'seat of the spirits' and is a spiritual focus in most Japanese homes. In one way it serves the same purpose as the mantelpiece in our western homes where we have a tendency to keep pictures of loved ones, ornaments and mementos from important times in our life. In Japan the Kamiza is a constant reminder of the family's historical legacy. In the dojo it serves the same purpose. The Kamiza, however, also serves a more spiritual purpose, which is to pay respect to the Kami or spirits of Nature. Most Kamiza contain the following symbolic items:

a rope to designate a revered place

candles to symbolise the universal cosmic light, of which we are a part

a mirror to inspire an 'unstained' heart and to represent self-reflection

tree twigs and branches to remind us we are part of Nature

dishes of salt or rice to symbolise willingness to sacrifice in order to grow and gain in our capabilities.

Wooden plaques with goals, wishes or the thanks of visiting students on them are often hung nearby.

As Master Norris finished his description I found myself drawn to the opposite wall on which were three magnificent Japanese paintings. Something about them and their positioning fascinated me. It was as if they were of the utmost importance and symbolic value. The first was of a figure in a wonderful orange robe sitting on a rock in meditation. The second portrayed an enigmatic figure with a rolled-up scroll in his mouth, holding his hand in a mystical position as he floated over a depiction of a toad. The third painting was that of a figure standing under a waterfall, again with his hand in a mystical position. The water was beating down on his body and he was struggling to resist its coldness and pressure.

James Norris explained that these pictures show the three traditions that influence our Ninja art.

Zen Buddhism

"The first shows Bodhidhamma, the founder of Zen Buddhism."

I knew that Master Hayes had trained in the Japanese Myoko Buddhist path and that he taught via a school called the Blue Lotus Assembly.

"Bodhidhamma founded his branch of Buddhism in China in AD500 at the Shaolin Temple. His school of Buddhism has a focus on meditation and self-control through insight. When his teachings came over to Japan they were protected by the Ninja families and embraced and incorporated into their own wisdom."

I wondered how much of the Chinese Kung Fu had come over with these teachings. Perhaps if they had, I would find some of the lessons easy to follow. It is from this tradition we get mind and spirit sciences and techniques of cultivating our unlimited physical, mental, emotional and spiritual potential. Through meditation and mind-correction methods we can learn skilful ways to transform the inner and outer challenges of life into success.

Ninjutsu

This represents the native Japanese Ninja warrior tradition. The figure on the toad is Jiraiya – in English his name means 'young thunder' – the title character of the Japanese folktale 'Jiraiya Goketsu Monogatari' ('The tale of the gallant Jiraiya'). Jiraiya is the archetypal Ninja. His stories are full of mystical power and cunning.

"What does the toad signify?"

"Well, Martin, it has many layers of meaning. Just like we have the saying 'as cunning as a fox', the Japanese have a saying that the toad is cunning and resourceful. However, here you see that the man is riding the toad. So it could mean that he has taken on the power of Nature or dominated the power of Nature. For the Ninja, uniting with Nature and using the knowledge of the nature of things held the greatest might, for if you are at one with Nature and part of all things, who can defeat you?

"There is also a story in Japan about how to keep a toad in a basket. If you have a hole in your basket and you want to carry the toad home without it escaping, you should make two other small holes; then the toad will keep trying to escape through a different route. He will try one hole and then if that's not easy, he will try the next and keep moving on. If there is only one hole, he will simply work at it until he is free. So in many ways the toad could represent our enemy, whom we defeat by our use of cunning; we overcome his nature by working with his nature."

"Could this also represent the controlling of the animal in ourselves?"

Master Norris seemed pleased.

"Yes, I guess it could. You see, the paintings have many levels of interpretation, each one with value depending on where you are on the path at the time."

It was this quintessentially Japanese tradition that produced the Ninja combat methods of the legendary phantom warriors born of Mount Togakure. From the woods and marshes of the shadowy Iga region came the core of our To-Shin Do physical protection techniques and strategies.

Yamabushi

"The third picture depicts a follower of the Shugend or Yambushi way."

The Yamabushi follow a path called Shugend , an ancient Japanese religion which literally translates as 'the path of training and testing'. The focus or goal of Shugendō is the development of spiritual experience and power. Yamabushi means 'he who lives in the mountains'. The whole path centres on an ascetic, mountain-dwelling lifestyle and incorporates teachings from Koshintō (ancient Shinto), Buddhism and other eastern philosophies. These ascetic mountain priests are part of an ancient tradition involving the practice of strict and rigorous mystical disciplines to cultivate psychic and spiritual powers. This is a special path whereby the followers believe that spiritual attainment can be gained through the mastery of the five elements of Earth, Water, Fire, Wind and Void. They test their will and develop self-mastery through trials involving the elements. Here you see depicted their most famous training method: standing under a waterfall and learning to control the pain.

From this tradition we draw the mind control and spiritual intention-channelling training of methods to aid our students to achieve a more focused and disciplined understanding of the cause and effect dynamics that lead to success and fulfilment in life.

At that moment it hit me; I had found it – a genuine Ninja school. Everything he said about the path rang true. I had touched the 'something' that I had been trying to reach through the darkness. This was exactly it! I was overjoyed!

"Anshu is here."

And there he was, Master Stephen K. Hayes. A tall, bearded man, he had a very relaxed manner. Something in him reminded me of my master Bo back in England, but I couldn't put my finger on what. As we made our introductions Stephen said something. Something subtle but very interesting.

"Martin, I want you to know that I'm impressed. Lots of people talk about coming, but very few do. I am genuinely impressed!"

With that, Stephen informed me he was going to be out of town for a few days but not to worry; we would get plenty of time together. In his absence I would be under the guidance of Master James Norris. And then, true to his name, 'the Haze' disappeared!

What had struck me so hard concerning his comment about being impressed was that he had read me so easily. From some email correspondence and 5 minutes conversation he had hit the nail exactly on the head. I came here with the intent to impress. How did he know? He could have said anything: *Welcome to Dayton; I think you will learn a lot. We are going to make a man out of you!*

But I didn't have time to analyse things too much as my first lesson was about to start.

The Five Elements

"Ninja training in To-Shin Do is based on the Five Elements. The Ninja concept of the five elements comes from the spirit influences we talked about earlier. In Japan the five elements are called godai ( ) which means 'five great'. Each element represents an archetypal state of being present in all levels of existence. They offer a classification system for the scheme of totality. The names of the five elements are (Chi) Earth, (Sui) Water, (Ka) Fire, (Fu) Wind, and (Ku) Void.

Earth

"Earth is the most dense and heavy of the elements and represents the hard, solid objects of the world. The most basic example of the earth element is in a rock. Rocks and stones have inertia; that is to say they are highly resistant to movement or change. In our personalities emotionally, Earth also represents this quality of stability in all forms. We instinctively use the elemental classification for some types of people. You have heard the sayings 'salt of the earth' or 'solid as a rock'. In England, I am told, they call someone who is really reliable 'a brick'. You see, we all instinctively know about the elements.

"The Earth type of personality is stable and solid. This could be manifested as stubbornness, mental stability, persistence. It also manifests itself as practicality, physicality and perhaps athletic ability.

"In the mind, it is confidence; emotionally it is a desire to have things remain as they are; a resistance to change. When under the influence of this Earth mode or 'mood', we are aware of our own physicality and sureness of action. Physically in our bodies the bones, muscles and tissues are associated with the Earth element. We all use the Earth approach to varying degrees in life. Some of us find it easier than others."

Water

"Water represents the liquid, flowing, changeable and formless things in the world. The best natural example of this would be a river. As with the other elements, there are sayings that have evolved to express aspects of this elemental personality. Have you ever heard the terms 'soppy', 'drippy' or 'wet' used to represent an overly emotional person? The Water personality type is represented by emotion, movement, defensiveness, flow, adaptability, flexibility, suppleness. Physically this element manifests itself in muscle flexibility, co-ordination, grace and fluidity of movement. In our physical bodies blood and other bodily fluids are categorised under the Water element."

Fire

"Fire represents energy and forceful energy-releasing matter; the roaring fire or the lightning strike epitomises this aggressive element. Physically Fire represents the heat of the body and the electricity in our nerves. We have all heard of someone who has been referred to as a fiery person, a firebrand or fire cracker. Someone is said to have a hot temper or to have had a heated argument. We talk about people being warm when they are friendly and cold (Water) when they are distant. The Fire personality is characterised by ambition, drive and passion. They tend to be dominating, outgoing and aggressive."

Wind

"The Wind element represents things that fill space and enjoy freedom of movement. Of course, air, smoke, steam and all gasses represent this element. It can in some ways be best represented by the human mind. A Wind type of person is optimistic, knowledgeable and logical. Someone with too much air element may be said to be spacey or an air head. People who talk too much are said to be 'full of hot air'. In our bodies it represents breathing, and all internal processes associated with respiration. Mentally and emotionally, Wind represents an *open-minded* attitude and carefree feeling. It can be associated with will, elusiveness, evasiveness, benevolence, compassion and wisdom. Wind in us represents our mind which like wind is free and creative. The Wind personality represents the outwitting of the opponent."

Void

"Void represents things beyond our everyday awareness; potential things, the quintessential creative energy. In fact in the western world we may call this element 'spirit' or 'ether'.

"In the physical body, this element represents mental force and creative energy, our ability to think and to communicate, as well as our creativity, inner strength, willpower, spontaneity and inventiveness.

"Void is the highest of the elements. This shows how spiritual values should come above all other material things such as power (Fire), knowledge (Wind), emotions (Water) or possessions (Earth). In martial arts a warrior who has mastered the Void element can fight without thinking, respond to situations spontaneously and intuitively and overcome all other opponents.

"In your time in Dayton we hope to give you an introduction to the first four of the elements. I don't want to go into the philosophy of the elements too much now. The real depth of understanding can only really be achieved by using the elements and practising their responses. The first level of To-Shin Do training is to learn the Earth-level response. This will be the focus of your first week of training."

Lessons of the Earth Element – Mountains of Strength

"Each To-Shin Do fighting technique can be classified by one of the elemental manifestations. The fighting system is taught as a total method of self-protection that includes defence against the most common form of attack and the building of skill that in time will lead to the ability to adapt to and deal with confrontation. The strategy and mental outlook for Earth level is that of solidity and strength. You hold your ground solidly; you are so firm that no matter what the onslaught it will not affect you. You know that your strength will prevail. Your adversary feels as though he is fighting against a rock impervious to anything he does."

I had spent the evening reading the training manuals issued by the dojo. I already knew what Master Norris had explained to me. I nodded in agreement, trying not to show my impatience.

Shizen no Kamae

"OK. Now here is your first Kamae or attitude position."

I was confused: he was just standing there. This was no martial arts stance. So I just copied and stood in a natural standing position.

"Correct! A Kamae is a position that represents the fighting attitude. The natural standing posture of the human body. Mind is alert, body is relaxed and ready to move and adapt to any situation. The body weight is equally distributed by both legs, the shoulders are down and the arms hang naturally at the sides.

"From this natural posture are developed the most sudden attacks and defensive actions. In this case it is stability and strength. Your opponent is not a challenge. Your attitude is: 'I am as strong as the mountain.' "

I was completely thrown. I could understand the need to be able to fight and respond from a normal standing position, but I actually felt very vulnerable from this stance and not at all ready for any martial arts action. However, as Master Norris started to take me through some basic movements I began to understand more about his Ninja art.

It occurred to me that the Kamae or body postures of Ninjutsu Taijutsu were more than martial arts postures or utilitarian stances. Unlike other martial arts that have formal ways of positioning feet or artificially holding the trunk, the Kamae of Ninjutsu are perhaps best described as the physical embodiment of a mental outlook, for they reflect the Ninja's heart. In any living or fighting situation, we naturally position the body in line with our consciousness. In Ninjutsu we work with Nature, believing that in order to be the most effective in any situation, the mind and body should be totally in tune.

As I practised I began to realise that the mind and body were so interlinked that mental division only caused problems. My mind was affected by my bodily positioning and vice versa. In actuality, there is no 'mind' and 'body'. These are terms that we apply to create divisions of one single entity. A change in your posture causes a change in your attitude. I realised that if I had truly known the Earth attitude I wouldn't had felt such impatience. The uncomfortable feeling in this posture was an indication of my inability to use the Earth approach to the situation – something that was becoming far more obvious as my training progressed.

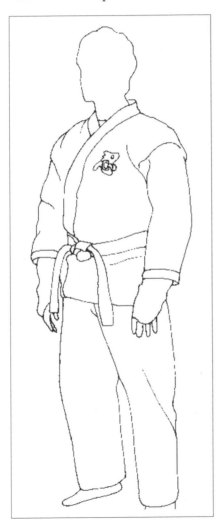

In each class I attended the routine would be the same. A combat situation would be the subject of the class. The attack would be something real, something that happens all the time on the streets. The response would be something simple but devastatingly effective. In fact what first struck me about To-Shin Do was how amazingly practical it was. I had never in all the twenty-five years of my martial arts career seen anything so effective.
(See fig.17)

Earth Defence Against a Straight Punch

In To-Shin Do you train to learn to respond to the attacks you are most likely to encounter in real life – punches, kicks, grabs and tackles – but the way modern thugs do them, not in a rigid or traditional way. The first thing that struck me about these methods was how

Fig.17

practical they were, how devastatingly practical but also simple enough that I knew I could use them in a high-adrenalin situation. The whole system is based on what Master Hayes calls the '5 Ds':

Discern, Defend, Disrupt, Deliver, Discern.

Your first challenge is to *discern* what the attack is. This, of course, is a process that starts from the moment you encounter your would-be attacker, calculating if this man is a threat or just crazy. Is he really going to attack? The moment an attack is launched you need to be able to respond. Your first response is to *defend*; then you need to do something to take his focus away, you need to strike him or otherwise make him off balance enough to *disrupt* his focus. Then you need to *deliver* a series of devastating attacks to neutralise his ability to be a threat. Of course, the fight may not then be over. So you go back to *discern*. Is he really out cold? Is he still a threat? Are his mates about to join in?

The defence against a straight punch is a good example of this: it starts with you standing normally in *Shizen no Kamae*.

(See figs.18,19,20,21)

The opponent launches his punch at you with either of his hands. In this case we have illustrated the attacker using his right fist. *(Discern)*

You respond by sinking and a slight parting of the legs into a natural ready position while immediately blocking his arm with your right palm as pictured. *(Defend)*

You then deliver a palm strike to his face while shouting, "Stop!" *(Disrupt)*

And follow up with a knee strike, again with a loud, "Stop!" *(Deliver)*

You finally push the opponent way with both hands while shouting, "Stay back," returning to your ready position. *(Discern)*

These drills and ones like this would be performed constantly at the Quest Center. There were no forms or flashy movements, just practice with a variety of opponents of all shapes and sizes. The aim was that in the end you would be able to defend any common attack from an opponent without being warned as to what was going to happen. After all, a mugger won't give you any warning! To achieve this we needed to learn to do things under pressure. But there was more than just practice!

Pressure Testing the Art

"Give me your money!"

His muscles tensed with raw anger.

"What's up with you? Do you have a problem?"

He grabbed my T-shirt and started pulling me around, raising his fist to attack. Rage and fear overcame me. I sprang into action. I had failed again.

Fig.18

Fig.19

Fig.20

Fig.21

During class we would practise the attack and our responses and at the end we would be tested by one of the head instructors, a large muscled man called Shane Stevens. Shane is the most positive person I have ever met. His whole being crackles with enthusiasm and energy. This energy, however, could also be intimidating if he chose to use it and at the end of each class we would be asked to demonstrate our ability to defend ourselves against an attacker in a real-life situation. The realism of these role plays had to be experienced to be believed. As soon as you are up on that mat with Master Stevens, it's real to him and that makes it real to you! No smiles, no fun, no games. It was through this testing I realised how limited my adaptability was. I only had one gear when approached by an attacker. Attack back!

It was so frustrating. Every day I would meditate on the Earth element. Every day I would work so hard to become that element. To hold my ground calmly and to apply the techniques as taught. As soon as I was put under pressure I would either find myself laughing and trying to lighten the situation or going to pieces and attacking aggressively – both of these being Fire element tactics. I noticed this was true of other areas of my life too. All my success in life had come from charging into things with great force. If that didn't work, I just applied more force. If I was to get anywhere with this art, I was going to have to learn to change.

The Ninja Attitude

It was at this stage in my development that I learned something from imitation of others, the examples set by others. One thing which is hard to express, which I learned in my time in Dayton, was that Stephen Hayes and his students really lived their art. They always seemed to be aware, full of cunning, and full of direction. I noticed they naturally walked far more silently than others. Everything they did appeared to be an exercise in discipline and self-development. Their calmness in the meditation hall extended into everyday life. The elements they were teaching – Earth, Water, Fire and Wind – they were using, and adapting, in everyday life. They were really being Ninja, not just studying Ninjutsu.

No form of reading or meditation could replace watching this practical application of everything. This example of fully being the art, which I witnessed in Dayton, is something which will stay with me for the rest of my life.

The feeling, which is extremely hard to describe in a book, is absolutely one of the most important things I have ever experienced in my life. It is almost like being able to absorb *cunning* by example. The whole Ninja state of being is that of continually adapting to who and where you are, not just learning these skills but also applying them – taking them away from the lesson and assimilating them into yourself.

Study Books and DVDs

But I needed something more. I needed a way to get the big picture of what was being taught. I started to read everything written by Stephen Hayes and discovered the range of instructional DVDs he had produced. I was training for up to seven hours a day, so in the evenings I would often just lie in my hotel room, reading or watching the Stephen Hayes DVDs on my television set. These instructional lessons were wonderful, for although Stephen Hayes was not there during the day, through this medium I had hours of his tuition every evening. Most martial arts DVDs are just someone doing something in front of the camera. These are different. They are far more valuable. Somehow Stephen Hayes has found a formula for making the most efficient DVD instruction in the martial arts. Even now, four years after initially purchasing a whole range, I find myself learning new things from them. The range includes titles on almost every aspect of Ninjutsu, including a myriad of exotic weapons and even a series on the use of meditation for the martial arts. You can buy the whole range at www.toshindo.com. I can't recommend them enough. This book gives only an introduction to what is being taught. I honestly believe you could master the art working through the DVDs with a partner.

It was through these DVDs that I began to realise something about Hayes. Everything he did he fully dedicated himself to. He was learning to be the best teacher he could be, the best martial artist, the most developed person possible. He didn't hold back at all and his focus was on what was real and not on appearances or social status. After he had learned the Ninjutsu art from Grand Master Hatsumi he could have lived happily for the rest of his life on the wealth he had created. But his spirit was that of an explorer. He didn't rest. He went on to seek the greatest spiritual masters he could in Japan and Tibet. His words were so wise, and I began to realise that here in Dayton was a true spiritual master, an enlightened adept of the warrior arts. I had travelled across the world to learn from him and he had gone. Where was he? I wanted to see the real Stephen Hayes again, not just watch him on a DVD.

My classes were, however, still not going to plan. Here I was with many years of martial arts experience but I couldn't deal with an attacker calmly or firmly. I couldn't get the basics down, so Master Norris in our private morning sessions offered some assistance.

"One of our most powerful Ninja secrets is how to bring us into the correct psychological state to give us an advantage over our opponent. For this we use the *Kuji*."

I had heard of the *Kuji*, a legendary set of mystical hand positions that was said to be able to have miraculous effects, to control nature, read minds, and this was the stuff of legend. Was he really about to teach me this Ninja magic?

Chi Kuji Goshin-Go (Earth Energy Channelling Self-Protection Method)
It was possible for a Ninja to find himself in a situation whereby his opponent had the upper hand, held a physically superior edge over him, was bigger, better trained or better armed. Perhaps he was outnumbered or in another position of inferiority. But the Ninja warrior knew that almost every victory is first won or lost in the mind.

For this very purpose the Ninja warrior would possess a secret weapon, a technique that is legendary in the mystical lore of the Ninja – a set of secret hand-weaving techniques known as the *Kuji* – that allowed the

Ninja to channel his energy, focus his awareness and bring about victory when facing adversity. These secret techniques have been used by the invisible warriors for over a millennium and allowed them to direct their mind, harnessing the most appropriate state of consciousness to gain success.

Many people believe the *Kuji* energy channelling process is simply a superstition or some form of Japanese cultural conditioning. It is, however, as I found out, something far more down to earth and practical; it is a technique of focusing your entire being and gaining better control over yourself.

The whole technique is based on something called the *Sanmitsu* or 'triple secret' – the combined co-ordination of intention, tactics and action.

Kuji-in teaches us that we have three methods of influencing the world around us. Our actions, our spoken words and our thoughts can all produce results.

The Secret of Focused Intention

First you need to focus on your goal. This will require a complete acceptance that things need to change and that to make this happen you need to change what you are doing. "There's got to be a better way" needs to ring throughout your being. The next step is to imagine exactly how you wish to change your relationship with your surroundings. You must know what you need to become, in order to work more effectively with what fate puts in your way.

To centre this focus you need to create an inner picture that symbolises your new state. The symbolic image should be something that is relevant, motivating and appropriate to you. The more powerful, emotive and inspiring the visualisation of the 'you to be', the more effective the exercise will be.

To stimulate Earth-like qualities you could imagine yourself as a figure or image that represents strength and stability. In the Japanese culture the Ninja would have used a Shinto deity with these qualities. You need to find an image inside yourself that represents the positive qualities of Earth. Concentrate on whatever image is most effective for you. Imagine how it would feel if you were that epitome of strength and command. You could imagine yourself as a natural object like a mountain boulder or giant oak tree. If you feel a connection with animals you could imagine yourself as a grizzly bear or timber wolf.

The Secret of the Spoken Vow

You could also say something commanding in a low powerful tone to stimulate those Earth-like qualities you require to deal with the situation. Perhaps you could repeat the words 'Earth' or 'Strength', the traditional way being to use a form of breathing associated with this element. To do this, inhale slowly and deeply. Feel your entire torso expand. Make sure you have filled your lungs with air all the way from the base of your spine. Then, after a very short pause, exhale at the same pace; it may help to imagine your breath passing through your body like a breeze through a deep cavern.

The Secret of Embodied Action

Now comes the hand position so legendary in this technique. To trigger the Earth state of mind, form rings with the thumbs (Void element) and the little fingers (Earth element) of both hands. Entwine the two rings you have formed and touch the tips of the other fingers together. Hold your hand in a praying position in front of your chest.

All three of the above should be performed simultaneously. Form the symbolic image of your goal in your mind's eye. Inhale using the Earth breath while forming the hand position. You need to use all three methods as a tool to reinforce your intent. Energetically will your adoption of the Earth mind state. As you exhale, raise your joined hands up over your head and with your inhalation pull them back to your chest. With your next exhalation thrust your conjoined hands forward in front of your chest, inhale and return them to the position over your heart. With imagination, breath and action in unity, set your resolve and invoke your inner Earth power.

When we had completed the exercise I felt stronger, more solid. Something really had changed inside and I was grounded and calm. I felt like I had connected to something in me – the whole exercise was like summoning something from inside.

"Now remember, Martin, this is totally natural. All animals know how to fight instinctively. If you grab a dog by the paw, it will bite your hand. If you grab it round the muzzle it will claw at your hand to free itself. It knows instinctively what to do. It's not like it has a black belt in Dog Jitsu or anything!"

I laughed but understood his point exactly. The state he wanted me to reach was one of an integrated mind and body, my actions totally natural. I too have observed the movement of animals as they fight or interact with their environment. Only human beings seem to develop the need to be trained in a natural body motion. Norris, however, had another story to tell.

Little Dogs

"You, Martin, are going to have to find your own way of getting into this Earth mindset," said Master Norris. "It may be through this visualisation; it may be something else that you've used in the past. Maybe you can imagine a time when you have been solid. Or maybe you can imagine a fictional or divine figure that could make you feel this way. But this is an example of the kind of feeling I think you should be looking for. I want you to imagine a big dog. Have you ever seen a big dog in the park? And a little dog comes up to it, like a chihuahua, barking away: yap, yap, yap, yap, yap, yap, yap. Do you know what the big dog does?"

"No."

"The big dog does nothing. Do you know why the big dog does nothing?"

"Why?"

"Because it's a big dog!"

"I'd like you to think about the analogy of the big dog and the chihuahua, barking away and being very, very verbal. That is the state of mind I'd like you to contemplate."

I had experienced times like this, when someone had been aggressive and verbally attacked me. I found it very hard to ignore the allegorical chihuahua and not hit the person because if I let it go, afterwards I would have such rage and such unfinished business that it would hurt me inside. So I explained that the real challenge for me was learning how to deal with the situation after it's over.

"You see," Norris continued, "from a Ninja point of view, we just want the person to do what we want. We're going beyond pride, beyond normal convention. So many people lose the situation to try to win status over the person, or to prove that they're top dog, so to speak.

"Ninjutsu is about winning the war, even if the opponent doesn't realise that you've won. Even if you make the opponent think that he's won. So, for example, imagine that I'm in a bar. A guy approaches me wanting a fight. Maybe he knows about the martial arts school, and he hits me.

"Now what does he expect me to do? Hit him back, get angry, all sorts of things. Now here's one way that I can win the situation. I don't want to fight; I don't want to be called up in front of a police officer, or to risk anything. I could just hold my mouth in pain, 'Oh God, man, that hurt!' and walk out.

"And, you know, if he badgers me, or is offensive on the way back, I could say, 'Yeah, yeah. No, I don't want to fight. No, no, no.' Now my pride may be hurt, but I've gotten exactly what I want. I mean, I get hit more than that; I've paid people to hit me better than that guy has hit me.

"So it's just your pride that's getting in the way on many of these occasions. Sometimes appearing to lose, or appearing not even to know that the guy is being aggressive, can be a far more powerful position.

"The strategy used in the last example is more Water strategy as you'll learn in the future, but what I'm trying to explain is that part of this Earth lesson is learning not just how to overcome external aggression, or things trying to make you move out of your position, but also how to overcome those internal forces like pride and aggression, or indeed the urge to show that you're more powerful than the guy, or that you're the dominant person in the situation.

"That's a very important part of what we're offering here at To-Shin Do, because by learning to adapt in these different ways, we learn to be more balanced."

I understood exactly what Master Norris was saying. But the idea of losing a fight deliberately was very alien to me. This was my first encounter not only with the creativity of Ninjutsu strategy but also in the liberating focus on your true aims. The idea of deliberately letting an opponent think that he had won so that he would leave me alone went against instinct and natural reaction. But I could see exactly what the truth was. If I could learn to do this, so many situations in my life would improve.

In a way, the person being attacked has the power, because he can lead the opponent, pushing in any direction that he wants. It is only inside himself that he is completely in control.

Once again a member of Dayton Quest had said exactly the right thing at the right time. I had just started to turn the corner in my training. From that moment onwards I could become Earth in the mind, and my body would reflect that. I would be immovable both emotionally and physically. It was still a new skill, but I was getting better with each practice session. I was also finding myself better able to apply Earth strategies in everyday situations. However, this uncanny ability of knowing what I was thinking was starting to get rather spooky. How did Master Norris always know exactly what to say?

The Workings of a Ninja Clan

Something was not normal at the Quest Center: the black belts were too aware, almost unnaturally aware, of what was going on. The students, however, seemed either to be totally used to it or oblivious. I found, for example, that every time I had discussed a subject with someone before a private class, even though the instructor was not in the room, my questions would be answered in the next lesson. I began to wonder if the room was bugged! I also noticed that if I told one black belt something, everyone would know, almost like a hive mind. This made them amazing instructors. Because of this awareness they would adapt and even alter their language to aid in your development. I began to experiment to determine how this was working. For example, a couple of times I had been in the process of training with a partner and had asked a question or made a suggestion; uncannily, a few seconds later, the teacher would stop the class and demonstrate the answer.

I once talked to Shane Stevens about body building and within a day all the instructors I met started to use more physical terminology and talked of muscle memory and making the technique part of the sinews. They were adapting and talking to people in their own terms, almost moving into harmony with the person's world view.

As time progressed I gradually realised that three things were responsible for this almost superhuman level of adaptation. The first was awareness. They seemed to possess an almost superhuman command of the senses. For example, a couple of times when I was stretching, Master Norris startled me by just appearing behind me, so silent were his footsteps. I tried to return the favour unsuccessfully. The man could hear what a fox could not!

The second reason was communication. The *Shihan* (expert instructors) of the school worked like a single unit and communicated everything to each other in as quick and efficient a way as possible. This way they all knew what the others did; it was a kind of omnipresence.

The third reason is rather important – love. The instructors were not just going through the motions; they were really trying to teach you with all their hearts. They cared in a way I had never seen a martial arts class function. They were giving it their all.

How to be as Strong as a Mountain
The whole Earth approach was extremely foreign to me: standing the ground, and not taking action. Earth is almost the art of inaction, or maintaining the status quo. In To-Shin Do training, you verbally state your intent. When the person attacks, you actually say, "Stop! Stop! Stay back!" as you block and defend. This is something I have never seen in any other martial arts and initially found very uncomfortable but immediately saw its value. It clearly delineates in your mind, and the opponent's, exactly what the situation is. Also crucially if someone comes in on the altercation, they are not going to mistake you for the aggressor. They will see quite clearly that you are defending yourself, and this would

be very useful in a court of law later on when questions are being asked as to who the attacker and who the defender was. No one runs in to mug someone, shouting "Stop! Stop! Stay back!" But as I practised, I started to realise that this verbal expression of things had a greater significance.

First of all, when people try to attack you, they tend to start off by distracting you. They tend to ask you questions. They tend to insult you or try to make you angry or scared so they can take control of the situation. By having this inbuilt response of shouting "Stop!" or "No! Stay back!" along with your movements, you begin to give your opponent something to think about and to react to, and you block off this line of confusion, distraction or misdirection that these kinds of people tend to use on you.

But the verbal statement is also something more. I thought about the mystical hand position, and meditative techniques of transforming your state of mind, and realised that in To-Shin Do training you are applying all three of these principles: visualisation, action and verbal expression. We were getting ourselves in that 'Earth Solid' state of mind. You have to chase energetically any doubts from your mind. 'Nothing is going to move me.' The talk about the big dog not responding to the small dog barking at it had given me the right state of mind: that I was impervious, that this person wasn't a threat.

And the "Stop! Stop! Stay back!" was the verbalisation of the intent which feeds in a loop. I can hear myself, and because I'm willing myself to say it, it's a self-fulfilling prophecy that I become that solid, assertive person.

Finally, we have the embodied action, the action of sinking, and of using these Earth-style strikes, these solid stop hits, which will defend us against the opponent. As soon as I realised the connection between the techniques, and that actually this Ninja magic was the very essence of what Stephen Hayes' school was teaching, things started to get easier for me.

The whole Earth element is about sinking motions and being solid and grounded. Your focus should be on weight and heaviness and the strength which that brings. I began to be able to get into that mindset, and there were daily tests of Earth – times when the best thing to do was hold my position. It was hard and I knew it would take a lot of practice, but I was gradually able to improve my performance in the classes. Inside, I was becoming more solid, more resistant, more authoritative, unmoved by the opponent's aggression and emotions. I was the immovable force that the opponent was charging into. I had finally got it. I had learned how to apply the Earth element in myself.

I was ready for the next level of elemental training. My next week of study would focus on the defensive element of Water.

Lessons of the Water Element – Waves of Power

No one walks in America. They don't build pavements and the police stop you if you walk long distances. They must think you are mad or up to no good. The local police had got to know me by now, and after the first few days left me alone. But something interesting was about to happen. Making my way to the Quest Center one morning a figure in the distance appeared on the verge. Someone else was on foot and he was heading in the same direction as me. It was a tall, fair-haired youth with a rucksack. Was he a tramp, a fitness fanatic or a mugger? More interestingly, why was he walking?

It turns out he was Danish!

Rasmas was a student of Ninjutsu who had flown in from Denmark to train at the Quest dojo. As two fellow travellers, literally on the same quest, we became friends and pooled our resources. It was wonderful to have someone at my side who had also just discovered the delights of root beer and Taco Bell. But fate had also just supplied me with far more than a fellow tourist; it had given me a living critic who would say what the polite Americans would not.

As I got to know Rasmas I realised there were only two categories in his mind. Either something was awesome, or it sucked! No middle ground, no shades of grey and no subtlety.

Within days Rasmas had informed me that my *Kamie* sucked, that I came across as loud, arrogant and boastful, and that everyone thought I was a liar. The terrible truth was that when I took time to analyse what he said, I realised he was totally right on all points. On landing in America I had done everything I could to explain to everyone I met how amazing I was and what amazing things I had done or was going to do. This strategy works wonderfully in my normal eccentric and elite social circles where I have a proven track record. With strangers in a different culture outside my understanding, it had failed completely. Contrary to cultural stereotypes, the Americans I had met had been polite, gentle and understanding whereas I had been brash, boastful and arrogant. Worst of all, I had not been able to match my big words with actions.

I knew I had a hard time ahead. I felt bad, but I just had to change my actions and keep learning.

Master Norris was starting the class.

Using the Water element strategy is about movement, shift and flow. You use distancing and unexpected movement to defeat your adversary.

You know that your fluidity and cleverness will overcome his brute force. Your opponent will feel like he is fighting the waves of the sea. You retreat from his advances and then crash back to knock him over.

The Kata for this element is as follows.

Ichimonji no Kamae

This classical Ninjutsu pose is the ideal starting position for sliding back and away to dodge an attack. Keep most of your weight on the rear leg. The leading leg is kept straight enough for the body to remain upright. Your shoulders should be relaxed and low. The lead arm is extended to keep a safe distance, while the rear hand protects the face and body as a shield. Point your lead hand directly at the opponent's eyes, with both hands ready to intercept the attacker's advance or to launch a counter-attack.

I had seen this position used before by Karl and Shaun and, though they never named it, I had used the footwork and understood something about the mechanics involved. I hoped that this would mean the Water element would come more naturally to me than the Earth element. *(See fig.22)*

Water Defence Against a Grab to the Chest

The Water element is all about fluid movement, angled zigzag footwork and using your superior scientific knowledge to defeat your opponent. Again all the attacks are against the kind of things you are likely to face in a genuine combat situation. The defence against a grip to the chest is the perfect example of this.

Your attacker extends his right hand to grab your chest, probably to pull you around or to punch you with the other hand. *(See figs.23, 24, 25, 26)*

You instantly respond by bringing your hands up to defend your face and by stepping back into the Ichimonji stance with your left leg. As you do so, use your weight and his momentum to pull him off balance; you should grab his hand and dig your right elbow into his attacking arm as pictured. You can also repeatedly strike the opponent with your right hand.

Next take a big step back with your right foot to reverse your position into Ichimonji on the opposite side. As you do, hug the wrist to your chest and use the turning of your body to twist him into a wrist lock. The movement uses your whole body weight to out-think rather than overpower the opponent. It is devastatingly effective.

It was about this time that I started to see the beauty of the whole

Fig.22

Fig.23

Fig.24

Fig.25

Fig.26

system. The same Ichimonji stance used to flow a person into a wrist hold is also used to evade attacks and gain leverage for countless techniques. This was something I could see had evolved over many hundreds of years to fit so perfectly. It is hard to convey in a book, but the training was not just a set of techniques. This technique is one of many different options that you learned to use naturally and adapt depending on what happens. One Ninja saying I heard repeatedly was: "One thousand changes, no surprises."

But combat wasn't all that was taking place at the Quest Center. A large amount of the curriculum was what was referred to as 'Mind Sciences'. Sometimes it was the mental adjustments the teacher would point out that needed to be made or the student should be aware of for the future. Sometimes it would be within the short contemplation on a certain subject at the start of the class. I found these all to be extremely useful and complementary to the physical teachings which were also leading insights, the scope of which would be beyond the space allotted in this book. But like any other martial arts school I have encountered, there were also specific classes on meditation.

Meditation for Martial Arts

The basic form of meditation practised at the Quest Center is an awareness meditation based on being in the 'here and now'. This form of meditation is very useful for martial artists because it teaches all the skills needed to keep your focus in a combat situation. Often during meditation practice you will find yourself distracted by external noises or things in the environment around you. With practice you will learn how to keep your mind focused, and even use distraction as a means of focusing your mind on your purpose.

This is an extremely useful skill in combat situations when a moment's loss of attention can lead you to defeat.

During meditation a large amount of distraction is internally generated and sometimes this is the hardest to control as it can be emotional and self-defeating. Of course, this skill is imperative for a warrior, who needs to remain in the moment without internal conflict or distraction destroying his focus.

And finally through meditation you learn to see things as they really are. You avoid being deluded and led into different alleyways. Just like our opponent may try to fool us into thinking the situation is different from what it really is, sometimes in meditation we feel we are in one state of mind when in fact we are not. It is not uncommon to spend 5 minutes thinking about tomorrow's shopping while fooling ourselves into thinking we are meditating. But before we can train our mind we need to find a calm stable position for our bodies to remain undisturbed in. In Dayton they recommended four different meditation postures.

HOW TO SIT FOR MEDITATION

Throne Posture
This posture is excellent for those who are unable or prefer not to sit cross-legged or in a kneeling position. It is the same pose that you will see depictions of Ancient Egyptian pharaohs sitting in: on a straight-backed chair (throne), feet comfortably placed flat on the floor and hands palm down on the thighs. Allow your shoulders to remain relaxed without slouching and your back firmly supported by the back of the chair, keeping your chin raised and the spine erect.

Burmese Posture
This is one of the best meditation postures in existence and one I was completely unaware of before I visited the Quest Center. For years I was using more complicated postures and found that after long periods my legs were numb. I also found it annoying that often I had to meditate when travelling or pushed for time and didn't have time to warm up. This posture, very common in Japanese Zen practice, is a simple position to master compared to the traditional Lotus posture and will be of use to you for the rest of your life. It also stretches the hips and opens them in preparation for the Lotus posture. In Burmese posture the legs are not crossed or the knees turned outwards to the floor. The legs are bent and the feet placed in front of the pelvis with one foot in front of the other. The hands rest at the top of the thighs or on the heels. Feel free to adjust the position of the feet until you are comfortable; it is perfectly acceptable to have the feet either straight in front of each other or to let them pass so that one foot is next to the other ankle. You may also have to adjust the angle to allow you to place your calves or knees on the floor.

In the Burmese posture you must pay attention to keeping your legs on the floor. When you cross your legs in Full or Half Lotus the knees are naturally pushed down. Not so with Burmese posture. It may take a while for you to sit comfortably in this position. To begin with you may not be able to rest your legs down comfortably, but don't worry about this as you will find that this improves with practice. If you are already practising meditation, I advise you to convert to the Burmese posture. *(See fig.27)*

Half Lotus Posture

This is the posture all the masters used for meditation at the Quest Center.

To begin, sit in the Burmese posture, then pick up your right foot with both hands, bringing it up into the cradle position. Sit in a relaxed upright manner. Place the right foot in the crease formed by the left thigh and the upper body. Adjust the left foot forward until it sits comfortably under the right knee. Your right leg should now be in a tight Half Lotus. Adjust your position so you can sit erect.

If your knee does not rest comfortably on the left foot then gently press down with your right hand. Hold the stretch for 30 seconds or so and repeat. Never bounce your knee up and down. Repeat with the other leg.

Don't worry if both knees don't rest on the floor or mat. Time will remedy that in due course. *(See fig.28)*

Full Lotus Posture

Sit with your legs straight out before you, on a cushion or folded mat to elevate the hips and allow the knees to sink through hip rotation. Keeping the back upright, bring your right leg into the cradle stretch position and externally rotate the right hip. Keep the right foot flexed, which helps prevent rotation at the knee and ankle joints. Place the right foot on top of the left thigh.

Relax the whole right leg. Now slowly bend the left knee in towards the folded right leg. Cross the leg in front of you. Pick up your left foot and lower shin and gently lift it onto the right thigh. You have now completed the pose. The left knee may be slightly above the floor. Relax; with practice this will even up. Continue to sit in a balanced upright position. The ideal position is not hard to find; just watch your breathing and position yourself where it is most free and easy. Either rest the hands on the knees with the palms facing up or hold them together on your lap. Start by staying in the pose for brief periods, increasing your stay as your hips increase in flexibility.

When your legs grow tired, stretch them straight out before you and gently massage your knees. Cross your legs the other way around and practise on the other side. *(See fig.29)*

How to Meditate

The meditation starts with an awareness of the breath. Move your mind to your breath and let your whole body relax with every exhalation.

After observing your breath for a while with each exhalation, start to repeat the word 'Here'. As you exhale repeat the word 'Now'.

Continue with your double mantra. Every time you breathe in repeat

Fig.27

Fig.28   Below: Fig.29

the word 'Here', then let your body exhale as you say 'Now'. There is no need to say either of the words out loud; just hear them in your imagination.

Make these words your focus and avoid getting pulled into other thoughts. You may find that, to start with, your mind tries to interrupt the process with all sorts of planning, evaluations and distractions. If you find at any time you have drifted off, don't criticise yourself for thinking or let yourself get frustrated. Just become aware of your distraction and move your mind back to that 'Here' and 'Now'.

Use your breath and the mantra to keep you connected to the present moment. Don't let yourself drift off or snooze. Keep your mind on your breath and the mantra.

This meditation is the first step in understanding how we can direct our internal experience, and in learning and understanding our unconscious habits. Soon you will notice what things disturb you and what things prevent you from being able to meditate effectively. Each time you notice a pattern, you have found something out about yourself.

As you persist with meditation you will find a wonderful state of calmness associated with the practice. It is a calm awareness. Don't expect or indeed look for a transcendental state of bliss. This calm feeling is known as the 'relaxation response' and carries with it many valuable health benefits including stress prevention, regulation of blood pressure and an improved immune system. You may also find that this meditation produces a mental clarity and a sense of well-being.

It is suggested that you practise for at least 20 minutes daily. If you can't manage 20 minutes straight away, try aiming for 5. This may seem like nothing, but make sure you can actually commit to this before you set grander goals – a small amount is better than none at all.

This form of mental training is one of the most important in the modern world in which more of us die from stress-related illness than violence or disease. If you consider how much of a battle in a survival situation is mental, it is amazing how it is all but neglected in other modern martial arts systems.

Sui Kuji Goshin-Go (Water Energy Channelling Self-Protection Method)
Of course the Ninja energy channelling exercises were also part of what were referred to as the 'Mind Sciences', and I was about to learn the second of them, in this case, the one for the element of Water, which of course uses the same triple secret as previously taught.

The Secret of Focused Intention
To stimulate Water-like qualities you could imagine yourself as a figure that represents responsive adaptability and cunning. In the Japanese culture the Ninja would have used a Shinto deity with these qualities, but just like you did with Earth, you need to find an image inside yourself that represents the positive qualities of the element. Concentrate on whatever image is most effective for you. Imagine how it would feel if you were that epitome of Ninja misdirection and cunning, using your mind to flow around and out-think your opponent. You could imagine yourself as a natural phenomenon like an unstoppable river or like the waves of the sea retreating and then crashing back. If you feel a connection with animals you could imagine yourself as a fox using his cunning to evade and outwit his opponent, or as a dolphin twisting and turning through the water.

The Secret of the Spoken Vow
The traditional way is to use a form of breathing associated with this element. To do this, inhale fully and deeply. Feel your entire torso expand. Make sure you have filled your lungs with air all the way to your lower abdomen. Then exhale quickly and forcefully. Imagine your breath like a wave withdrawing slowly, building up its strength and then rebounding on a cliff face with great force.

The Secret of Embodied Action

To trigger the Water state of mind, use the legendary hand position to form rings with the thumbs (Void element) and the ring fingers (Water element) of both hands. Entwine the two rings you have formed and touch the tips of the other fingers together. Hold your hand in a praying position in front of your chest.

All three of the above should be performed simultaneously. Form a symbolic image of your goal in your mind's eye. Inhale using the Water breath while forming the hand position. You need to use all three methods as a tool to reinforce your intent. Energetically will your adoption of the Water mind state and breathe in. As you exhale, thrust your joined hands up over your head then, as you exhale, pull them back to your chest. As you exhale, thrust your conjoined hands forward in front of your chest, inhale and return them to the position over your heart. With imagination, word and action in unity, set your resolve and invoke your inner Water power.

Independence Day

In the United States, Independence Day falls on the 4th of July. It's a big national holiday and everybody attends firework parties, has barbecues, parades, picnics and generally has a good time. For the American Joe Public, this is a wonderful day. It represents their becoming free of an oppressive foreign power. For an Englishman in America, it's a rather uncomfortable event because basically this is a celebration of when they beat us in a war.

Independence Day for me, however, was very exciting. I had been taken in by an American family called the Griffins. Most of the Griffin family attended Dayton Quest, and they took pity on Rasmas and me, left alone in our hotel rooms while everyone else had a good time. We attended a spectacular firework display and then were treated to some good old-fashioned American cooking. The family's blood comes from Ireland; maybe that's why there was such a wonderful sense of warmth between the members of the family. Rasmas was full of happiness and really seemed to feel at home.

But my mind was also on higher matters. Where was Stephen Hayes? How was I going to advance in this path? And as most of the members of the family were on the same path, I took time to ask them questions. As we discussed things, I realised that one very important difference between how I was approaching my Ninja art and how they were, was to do with personal responsibility and independence. Perhaps because of my previous martial arts training or perhaps because of something in my nature, I was relying heavily on the teacher to be the driving force behind my personal development. I wasn't independent.

It hit me at that precise moment; the one very important thing that Stephen Hayes was teaching me by not being there was that you cannot rely on anyone but yourself for your personal development. The lessons were all in front of me. I just needed to embrace them. I needed to let go of my reliance on him and take personal responsibility for everything I was doing, which is something that the students at Dayton Quest had achieved.

During the conversation, we talked about another senior instructor called Richard Sears. They were talking about how he had recently gone away on a retreat and had undertaken some Yamabushi training under a waterfall. I was overwhelmed. So these trials that Stephen Hayes mentioned were actually being done by modern-day practitioners of To-Shin Do. What dedication. What inspiration. I knew I was exactly amongst the right people to gain the knowledge that I needed.

As we continued to talk, something else inspired me. It dawned on me that there was something else extremely different about this martial arts class from other classes or communities that I had seen before. Everybody could take part. Now many martial arts tell you "anyone can try", but it's not true. You very rarely find anyone with a disability in a martial arts class. In Stephen's class, there are some spectacular examples of perseverance and achievement through adversity.

One training partner that I had been fighting with that very day actually had a completely false leg. He had obviously had an amputation at some point and I only knew at the end of the class when he explained to me. I did notice during the class that he kicked only with one leg, but hadn't connected what the cause was. There was also a man who used to be a power lifter whose shoulder had been so damaged he could barely lift his arm above shoulder level, and one of the senior instructors, Shane Stevens, who we met earlier, was going blind.

Shane deserves a special mention here because despite having quite a hard background in life, and indeed his degenerating eye condition, you would never notice anything but joy, happiness and encouragement. I think that many of the great achievements in that class were due to the involvement of this man. Every morning Shane would be there with a wonderful beaming smile on his face, full of positive encouragement, and there was just something about him that made you feel you could overcome anything.

Right there, sitting at the Griffins' table, I realised that there were people in the class who were fighting far harder to be there than I was and were overcoming far more difficult situations than I. This place was full of real Ninja; people who could endure and persevere through anything, and this independence, this endurance, was inspiring beyond compare. This was the *Nin* in Ninjutsu. I decided to take this lesson with me for the rest of my life and to never again rely on another person for my personal development.

How to Fight Like the Waves

To fight like the crashing waves of the sea, one has to be as soft and receptive as water. Water is the softest thing and because of its softness nothing can hurt it. Yet with its eroding force or the colossal strength of a tidal wave it can also be extremely deadly. The To-Shin Do Water strategy is based on the ability to retreat and either use the attacker's force against him or rebound with tremendous energy. When we first started to practise these techniques I noticed everyone was dodging far faster than I was. It took me a few hours of practice to realise the essential difference. I was stepping while everyone else was performing some form of controlled fall. The Ichimonji stance allows you to create a very sudden and yet controlled retreat by simply lifting your rear leg and letting your body weight carry you. This allows you to respond and indeed move far faster than any other martial artist who has to take a step. During this period I began to appreciate that one of the amazing powers of this martial art school was the amount of time focused on the really effective basic movements. Never in my martial arts career had I had to dodge block so many strikes, and with every hour that passed I knew I was getting better. The Water feel came far more easily to me. Fluid-calculating adaptability defeated the stronger or better armed opponent. I had experienced my second element, but where the hell was Stephen Hayes?

The Fire Element Lesson – Lightning Strikes

"When working with the Fire element, you fiercely and aggressively pursue your adversary. The more he struggles, the more powerful your blows become. It's like you're a roaring fire: the more he struggles against you, the hotter you become. Your opponent feels as though everything he does just fans your flames, making you hotter and brighter with each action he makes. The solar plexus is the body's centre of motion and consciousness."

As Master Norris said this, he clenched his fists and lifted his hands into a cross in front of his body.

Jumonji no Kamae

In this position both arms cross at the wrists slightly to protect the body during advancing attacks. The elbows cover the rib cage and the fists cover the neck and face. The body weight is maintained with a slightly forward balance and the feet push the body solidly in the attacking direction; both feet are angled forwards.

I adopted the position. It felt powerful and full of explosive energy, like a boxing stance. I was excited to be about to experience some techniques in my natural element. *(See fig.30)*

Fire Defence Against a Kick

When I first started working with the Fire element I was full of energy. I thought the whole principle was about exploding with rage and energy. However, nothing could be further from the truth. The Fire strategy is about interception. Your blows are well-aimed missiles that fire off quickly, hitting the exact target with devastating effect. This requires focus and quickness, and a wonderful example of this is the Fire defence against a kick.

Your opponent starts to kick at you with his right foot.
(See figs.31, 32, 33, 34)

As soon as you realise the kick is coming you intercept with a swift step and punch, leading with your right arm and right leg. Your punch is aimed at the pit of the stomach on a downward angle. This totally stops the kick in its tracks, the whole force behind the kick being turned against the attacker, and he receives damage from both your striking power and from his forward momentum.

HI KUJI GOSHIN-GO (FIRE ENERGY CHANNELLING SELF-PROTECTION METHOD)

The Secret of Focused Intention

To become fire-like inside, you could imagine yourself as a figure that represents responsive forceful action and connection. To summon the inner fire visualise an image that represents positive qualities of Fire. Imagine how it would feel if you were the epitome of combat effectiveness moving faster than your opponent and with greater accuracy. You could imagine yourself as natural phenomenon like a bush fire or a lightning bolt. If you feel a connection with animals you could imagine yourself as a lion roaring or a cobra spitting venom.

Fig.30

Fig.33   Below: Fig.34

Fig.31   Below: Fig.32

The Secret of the Spoken Vow

The traditional way is to use a form of breathing associated with this element. To do this, inhale quickly and forcefully to the solar plexus. Feel your rib cage expand. Then exhale quickly and forcefully. Imagine your breath like bellows heating the flames within. Each breath raises the temperature.

The Secret of Embodied Action

The hand position for this technique is as follows. To trigger the Fire state of mind, form rings with the thumbs (Void element) and the middle fingers (Fire element) of both hands. Entwine the two rings you have formed and touch the tips of the other fingers together. Hold your hand in a praying position in front of your chest.

All three of the above should be performed simultaneously. Form your symbolic image of your goal in your mind's eye. Inhale using the Fire breath while forming the hand position. You need to use all three methods as a tool to reinforce your intent. Energetically will your adoption of the Fire mind state. Inhale then breath out as you lift your joined hands up over your head, then pull them back to your chest. As you exhale, thrust your conjoined hands forward in front of your chest, inhale and return them to the position over your heart. With imagination, word and action in unity, set your resolve and invoke your inner Fire force.

The Return of Stephen Hayes

I was about to leave after the class when, suddenly, there he was. Stephen Hayes was back.

I was very tired; I had been training for seven hours a day for two weeks. I was tired in a way that I had never experienced before. I had never skipped a class. I had never stopped practising. My pride hadn't let me. I really wanted to prove myself. And now that Stephen K. Hayes had returned to his dojo, I wasn't capable of performing my best any more.

Stephen seemed very happy to see me. But he was nowhere near as happy as I was to see him. We started our classes together but they didn't take a form I expected. Stephen was passive and responded to my questions rather than driving the lessons. He kept me off balance. I never really understood whether he was testing me or teaching me. A lot of things he was expressing I couldn't understand, and he changed direction often.

He would put me in different martial art positions or in different scenarios, almost as if to see what I would do. I found myself confused, pointed in many different directions, and my mind was continually searching for the purpose of whatever we were covering in the lesson. I don't know if it was the tiredness or whether this was a deliberate strategy.

I still think back to the lessons, and there are moments where messages that he was trying to get across suddenly dawn on me. But a lot of it was still completely misunderstood and confusing in my mind. In retrospect, perhaps I wasn't the best student to deal with. Sometimes, when Stephen was trying to demonstrate a technique, I would do my best to get out of it by trying to display my previous martial knowledge.

I did really want him to see me as an experienced martial artist, but I think this started to create a barrier between me and the new information he was giving me. Sooner or later, things came to a head. Stephen was demonstrating the technique, but I, as usual, was resisting and trying to show him how much I already knew. The whole situation began to disintegrate into a form of playful combat. I say 'playful combat' because for Stephen it was playful. For me, it was deadly serious.

I had fought many different martial artists from many different countries. Some of them were world champions known to be the most skilled men in the world, with great titles, belts and fame. Stephen Hayes, however, was a completely new experience for me. At 30 years of age, I was extremely physically fit. I had trained for an hour and a half in the gym every day for the last six years, and not many people had the kind of strength that I had.

When I fought Stephen, who was approaching 60, I didn't expect to have any problems when it came to overpowering him if it came to the crunch. But Stephen had a different way of fighting; one than I had never seen before. Everything he did was powered by me.

Initially, I tried to take him down by tackling him in what we call a single-leg takedown. It's a move from wrestling and from some of the Russian martial arts. I grabbed him on the leg, threw my shoulder into the top of his thigh and put my entire weight into toppling him.

I felt his leg buckle underneath me, and I knew that I had taken down the martial arts legend, Stephen Hayes. My martial arts style specialises in being on top of a grounded opponent. So I knew I had just moved him into the most dangerous area. However, something suddenly went wrong. A pain shot through both my arms. I was trapped and confused. Stephen Hayes had relaxed his entire body, turned his leg to the side, and let the leg that was being tackled collapse, catching my right hand underneath his shin against the ground, and my left hand between his thigh and lower leg.

It was something I had never seen done before. I had no idea that it would work in any way. I struggled to move my hands back, but Stephen was relaxed and calm. He didn't realise that this was a competition. He was just showing me techniques. As I tried to struggle free, I began to change tactics. I grabbed hold of his arm to pull him into an arm lock called an arm bar.

I knew that no one could get out of an arm bar, especially a man with less strength than the person performing it. I pulled his elbow right under my arm. I could see he was surprised by the action. I put all my body weight onto the arm and he started to fall towards the ground. I had won! He may have been able to get out of the tackle, but this arm bar was something I had specialised in since I was a small child.

Just after the moment of impact, Stephen's arms somehow melted away from underneath me. He bent his arm so it just seemed to disappear. Perhaps I had my arm slightly above the elbow, but it just went. I still had a hold of his arm, and I tried to hit him with my hand. Stephen, however, had other plans. He positioned his body in such a way that his whole body weight was behind his movements; he drew the arm I was grabbing downwards with such force that it pulled me off my feet. I could see that this motion was a simple matter of body positioning. But, because I was so overpowered, it seemed supernatural.

My strike missed; my wrist hold no longer existed and I had fallen off my feet. But I kept my grip on his wrist ready to pull him to the ground. He pushed a point on one of my fingers that caused a giant crunch and a click. It felt like my finger just disconnected. I had never seen anything like that before. I knew there were pressure points that could cause pain, but one that could dislocate a finger?

Stephen then moved my wrist into a lock, but I rolled out to escape the pain. He changed direction and I rolled again. Then something amazing happened. He used his leg to jam my arm and put me in a hammer lock. I had seen this kind of thing done in choreographed fights – but never with a resistant opponent. I was stunned. Stephen had been play-fighting with me, in the same sense that I would play-fight with a toddler. I looked at him and realised I had never met a martial artist like him before in my life.

I was completely outskilled and outclassed. I was in shock. I thought about my previous training and felt humiliated. I thought I had a firm base in martial arts skill, but I was wrong. At that precise moment, I also appreciated how right Rasmas was; I had been very boastful and arrogant. I had no doubt in my mind when I came to America that I would amaze everyone, whereas my performance had in fact been mediocre.

I was in such a state of shock that I found it very hard to pay attention to anything else for the next two days. Stephen could see what had happened. In fact I now believe it was something he may have planned. I had come over aggressive, boastful and full of myself. And Stephen had taken some time to observe me, gave me time to wear myself out, and then had come in and showed me the truth.

I didn't know if I was thankful or not. I really had to look at how tall this mountain I was about to climb was. Could I ever achieve the degree of skill that this man had? Could I actually do this? I found it extremely hard to be stable and found myself continually reflecting upon the situation. *(See fig.35)*

Fig.35

Breaking Down Barriers

My next lesson with Stephen Hayes was torturous. I was already broken from my previous combat and I found I was unable to do much at all. Stephen asked me to perform a step and a jab, a basic technique – perhaps the most basic technique in the whole of martial arts – and I simply couldn't co-ordinate it the way he wanted, something that had never happened to me before in my life.

Stephen said, "We should practise with a sword, just for fun."

But again, I found myself completely unable to do what he was showing me and again this was something I had never before experienced. Ever since I was a child I had found any physical skill really easy compared to others, but now I couldn't do what he said. This made me appreciate how much physical things are in the mind. It seems to me that the barriers are internal and not dictated by birth or talent.

We sat down and Stephen talked of stories. He told me of a man he once knew, a businessman, who would use his skill and intellect to dominate others. When the boss wasn't there he would use his intellect to bully people. Once his employer came back to the office early and waited, listening. In order to test him, he set someone up to ask him a question and listened to what he had to say. People who use intellect to bully can't resist it, and they are often unaware they are doing this.

I realised that the story was about me. When I had talked to one of the senior black belts a few days earlier he had asked me about the pictures on the dojo wall. I was surprised that he didn't know about them and had gone to great lengths to explain in detail everything I knew about them.

Stephen then moved on to a different subject. He talked of a businessman who once came to the Dalai Lama asking to buy enlightenment. The Dalai Lama had explained that enlightenment couldn't be bought. Once again, I realised the story was about me.

Stephen continued his parables. He talked of how animals tend to give away their weaknesses by how they respond; that they try to make themselves look bigger than they are, and that in humans this was true as well. The areas where people puff themselves up tend to be those where they feel the weakest. In doing so, people give themselves away and as Ninja we should all get past this.

Again the story was about me. However, as I looked at the other students in the class I realised that many people there were thinking that perhaps it was about them.

One of the interesting things about Stephen Hayes is that you never know if things happen by accident or on purpose. Like a true Ninja, he continually keeps you off balance. Did he go away in the early weeks deliberately so he could observe me from a distance and tire me out? Or was he simply going away for Independence Day? Had he set up the confrontation last night deliberately to test me? Or was it something that naturally occurred? This characterised Stephen Hayes' way of teaching. He would say things in such a way that people could grab and grasp it as a lesson, or completely ignore it if they were not ready. After the lesson Stephen took me to one side.

What You Really Want – Lightning Bolt to True Focus on your Goals!
"Martin, one of the most important things for Ninja and spiritual development is to know oneself. In order to control others' emotions, you must first be able to control your own. To control others' emotions, you must know what they're feeling. You can know how they would feel in any situation by putting yourself in a similar situation and by knowing what kind of person they are.

"To find your true motives, I'd like you to contemplate this. If you were to win or gain through inheritance millions of pounds and never have to work and struggle again, what would you do with that money? Would you spend it to glorify yourself? Would you use it to party and to have hedonistic fun? Would you give some away to help people? What would you do with the time you have on this Earth?"

It took me a few moments to think about this. I realised that, pre-Dayton, I probably would have spent the money partly, as he stated, on self-glorification. I probably would have spent some of it on fun, but I think something there had got my focus to the true essence of myself. I would use the money for two purposes: I would do good, and I would spend my life travelling the world, studying from the greatest spiritual masters and using my spare time to develop myself spiritually, mentally and physically.

Those are my true motives.

Stephen could see this had had an impact on me.

"Martin, in all things you do, examine your motives and keep focused on the true goal behind your undertakings. In this lies the greatest power."

Knowing my own motives and knowing what I really wanted from life made a difference, not then but in the future.

We all seek pleasure, power, dominance and prideful actions, but knowing how little these things really mean to you in the core of yourself, how little your financial success is of importance to you compared to your higher, real goals inside, begins to lessen their power.

It's almost as though by knowing your emotions you listen to them, and people who are listened to don't need to shout as loudly. I found in the weeks to come, my ability to negotiate with the negative qualities or controlling emotions within myself improved, and a strange feeling came over me, as if through the elements something was changing.

I was starting to see things in another way. It's a subtle thing, but I have found that ever since that talk I have been examining my motives in detail and that this has marked a gradual change in how I do and view things. It has also shown me how most people travel through life aimlessly, with no idea of what they are hoping to achieve. Let me try to explain.

Imagine a couple; let's call them Bob and Sandra. Bob loves Sandra and really wants to make her happy. He knows that she loves the zoo so he arranges for them to go the following Saturday. He also arranges for some of her friends to go with them. The day before he packs the car and makes them all a lovely packed lunch. He sorts the road map out and plans a route and generally gets everything ready. Bob likes to have things in order.

The morning of the trip arrives, but Sandra has a bad headache and is not in a good mood. Bob is not happy with how she is treating him over breakfast and Sandra knows she is being unfair, but the headache is controlling her mood. They get in the car and go to pick up her friends. She is suffering, her head is throbbing, Bob is fuming. How can she ruin everything like this? Can't she see the effort he has made? Why is she acting like this? They pick up her friends but the tension in the car is terrible. They turn up at the zoo and the atmosphere is terrible. They argue and everyone suffers throughout the day.

Now what went wrong? Well they lost focus as to what they were trying to do. If the aim was to get to the zoo no matter what, then they succeeded, but the aim was, of course, to make Sandra happy and have a good time. FAIL!

So what should Bob have done? First he should have managed her feelings that would be associated with the guilt of cancellation, called the whole thing off and pampered his headache girl all day. That would have made her happy. SUCCESS!

It is almost as though Ninjutsu is based on Buddhist enlightenment. What we all need is *Vajra*, a lightning bolt of self-examination. A powerful questioning: "What exactly do I really want?"

When you do this you begin to see that the world is full of people who are unhappy and miserable because they don't really know what they want. They are working hard to impress a father who is long since dead or long since impressed. They are stuck in a job that they joined to gain contact with people who are no longer there or for an enjoyment that has long since left.

When we see this in true view it opens up an amazing burst of creativity that allows us to aim directly at our goal without being caught up by our emotions or pre-set ideas of how things are done. It is this focus on our goals and reaching them, like a lightning bolt taking the shortest or most efficient route, that I believe is the essence of Ninjutsu and the reason why everything at the Quest Center is so effective. It is also the secret of the Fire element.

The Path of the Protector

The training in Dayton was directed towards modern-day life. As an Englishman, I found a lot of the gun training scary. We have more of a problem with knives; guns are things we just don't see in the street.

But it's important that we don't freeze if the unexpected does happen and, of course, I knew in the future I would have to travel widely, so this would be a very practical skill for me. However, during the training on the Fire elements, I began to see a theme developing.

The view of Stephen Hayes' martial art broadened for me and I realised that his vision was part of a dream – a dream that would change the world for the better. He wasn't just training fighters or thugs. He was training people in levels of development leading to them doing exactly what he did: protect people.

On the Earth level, you learn to hold your ground and defend yourself. By the time you are on the Water level of consciousness, you start to move and evade problems, and find different ways of dealing with situations. In the Fire element, you begin to protect others and can become a powerful force for good in the universe.

We can become a secret hero or protector – someone who will intervene when another needs help. Just like Stephen Hayes protected the Dalai Lama, who represents the sacred. We work to become secret protectors for everything that is sacred, for goodness, for love and for happiness.

This vision inspired me. This world needs secret heroes: people who, without anyone knowing, are there to help others. This dream helped me forge ahead at a time when I was in emotional crisis. It is an amazing ideal, and it made me think of a world where all dojos would have the moral direction and practical focus of the Quest Center.

How to Fight Like the Roaring Flames

The Fire element is based on interception, on connection and attack. Your attack is a lightning bolt that hits directly and quickly. The footwork is based on the opposite of the Water footwork.

Your body is in a ready position, with a slight lean forward, the weight predominantly on the front foot. As you lift the foot, your whole body moves forward with the power behind your lead punch. Once again, it's more of a controlled fall.

I had never seen this form of punching before and was quite surprised that I could get such force in a jab as strong as a traditional karate rear-handed punch, which gains its power from a turn of the hips.

That strike was devastating and I found I could use this fast forward motion with amazing effect. Much of the Fire technique is about pre-emptive striking. Your opponent is about to make an aggressive move and you connect with him with fast and powerful blows, disposing of him before he has time to think.

To fight like Fire, you need to be completely in the moment. It's not a rage, of going nuts or losing control; it's a pure connection with the moment. It's a forward moving, aggressive, swift force with great accuracy and zeal. I found this approach naturally very easy.

You need to imagine yourself like a back-draft or a roaring set of flames in a fire in order to move your awareness completely onto the destruction of your opponent. Every movement is an attack. If you need to dodge, your dodge becomes a stepping attack; this is the way of Fire.

One of the most valuable things about learning To-Shin Do is that you become aware of your existing strategies. I found that in the past I been using Fire strategies in almost every area of my life, even when perhaps other strategies would have been more appropriate. But my greatest challenge was waiting for me.

Lessons of the Wind Element – The Eye of the Storm

I had come to America seeking enlightenment and expecting it to taste of honey, to be a sweet and pleasant experience. In fact it was like vinegar. I sat there at breakfast, dreading the lesson ahead. I knew that I had failed and I knew that I had made a fool of myself.

Another person at the breakfast table went to fill up his cup of coffee. He had pressed the button on the coffee machine and initially it hadn't worked. He pressed it a second time and the coffee cup started to fill but then, not paying attention to what he was doing, he pressed it a third time.

The hot coffee spilled all over his hand, scalding him. He was trying to fill a cup that was already full. Then suddenly something hit me. I realised that I had been doing exactly that; I needed to empty myself. I had come here full of myself, full of knowledge and pre-existing ideas, but now I had to be like the void with an open mind, ready to absorb everything.

As I got to my lesson, there was a new attitude, a new way of being, a new feeling inside. Master Hayes opened the dojo door. "Ready to learn?" he said, with a smile.

And I truly was. Once again, Stephen really knew what was going on inside. We had to get rid of a lot of obstructions, but now it was time for the real lessons.

"Under the influence of the Wind level of the personality, you fight like a whirlwind of force. Your opponent strikes and there is nothing there. By the time his mind has updated your location, you have moved. You, like the Wind, keep the enemy off balance; you push and pull him so he is confused and unaware of where he is. Your focus is not on injuring him, but you use enough force to discourage without harshly punishing him. You turn everything he does against him and intercept his moves. You are so swift that you stun him without the necessity of blocking first. The centre of the chest is the body's centre of motion and consciousness, allowing for quick, light and spinning movements." Stephen moved his body into a kind of spread-eagle formation. It was one so natural that we had all probably used it when preparing for action. Once again, this was a position I had seen used before but which had never been named.

Hira no Kamae

To adopt this posture, take a wide stance and make sure that your weight is equally distributed between both legs. You should feel like you can move and pivot forwards or backwards on either foot at any movement. Your hands should both be wide open, leaving the chest exposed and presenting a big target on purpose, which both psychologically scares the opponent (as a cat makes itself look big to its enemy) and lures him to attack where you expect him to. This posture is amazingly powerful and, as with all Ninjutsu, the footwork is where the power is. *(See fig.37)*

Wind Defence Against an Attack from Behind

The Wind element is all about fitting in to the opponent and evading him. You use your closeness and speed to use his momentum effortlessly against him. Wind's movement type is rotational which makes it a harder element to master than the sinking stability of Earth or the zigzag flow of Water or even the linear interception of Fire. A good example of this is the Wind defence against an attack from behind.

The attacker approaches you from behind and either grabs or shoves you. *(See figs.38, 39, 41)*

You use the force and whirl in the direction of the force of his attack, sinking at the knees and raising your arms *Hira no Kamae* as you go. Use the turn to look at the opponent and, using your lead hand, strike his neck with Shuto sword fist. Use the natural momentum to follow up with knees or strikes, working with the direction of your turn.

Honing the Senses

Stephen and I sat in the Meditation Room. As we sat there it occurred to me how important meditation and mental control must be to Stephen's teaching for his dojo to have a room specifically for meditation.

Stephen began to talk.

"The awareness-development exercises of To-Shin Do training are complementary to the overall attitude of complete growth and realisation that are inherent in the art. As a comprehensive lifestyle, the Ninja regards the body and its sensual capabilities as tools for the accomplishment of life's purposes. As such, they are to be acknowledged for their value, well cared for, and fine tuned. The exercises that follow will help you hone and improve your senses and gain better awareness. Make sure you leave two or three days between your exercises so your consciousness has time to adjust."

Fig.37

Fig.38

Fig.39

Fig.41

Elemental Correspondences to the Five Senses
Earth – Smell
Water – Taste
Fire – Sight
Wind – Touch
Void – Hearing

Mastering the Sense of Smell – Earth Element

This exercise should be performed as soon as you wake at the start of the day.

Keep your eyes closed and focus on your sense of smell. It may be the subtle scent of fabric softener from your sheets or a stronger scent like that of food cooking. You may not initially be aware of any smell at all. Remain passive and breathe normally. Give yourself time to discover all the subtle scents you can detect. You may be surprised how after a few moments you start to notice more and more subtlety in what you are sensing – for example, the smell of the wood of the furniture or the window polish used yesterday. You will discover your sense of smell is far more sensitive than you thought.

Try to take this increased awareness with you during the day and use this in all that you do. Allow yourself to notice all smells.

Focus on all scents, whether you naturally like them or not; importantly use your sense of smell in all you do and don't just focus on obvious things that people normally assume are scented like flowers, perfume, etc. Notice the scent behind everything – note how your computer's scent changes when it is turned on, see if you can smell if your secretary has got into the office. Notice the smell of the paint as you walk down the corridor, or of a pencil when you write with it. If you find at any point your awareness has moved away from your sense of smell, bring it back to this focus and take a deep breath to explore your olfactory surroundings.

Mastering the Sense of Taste – Water Element

As you awaken at the start of the day, keep your eyes closed and remain still; allow yourself to acknowledge any tastes you notice. Open your mouth slightly and inhale, allowing the air to flow over your tongue. Give yourself a few moments to taste the air as a snake would. Bring this increased awareness into your life that day, keeping your focus on the sense of taste. You don't have to change your diet but when you do eat, focus completely on what you consume. Make sure you are not distracted by anything else around you and try not to engage in conversations or watch TV. Take time to sense the ingredients in everything you eat.

Mastering the Sense of Sight – Fire Element

This exercise is also to be performed as soon as you wake. However, in this exercise you should open your eyes and simply allow yourself to take in whatever is directly within your gaze. Try to take in everything you see; notice the shapes, the shadows and the forms. Experiment with how wide your vision is and the limit of what you can see. Notice the colours and the variations in their appearance due to the light. Shift your vision and focus to different areas of your scene. Blur your vision intentionally and see if you can adjust your focus to a variety of distances. Give yourself two minutes of focusing on your sense of sight and then take this awareness with you into the day. Throughout the day be careful to notice the effects of what you see. Notice how colours are used to create certain emotional effects in people and how this affects you inside. Try to look at each object or scene anew and analyse the effect it has on you and those around it. For this day the world is your art exhibit. You will be surprised what you suddenly notice happening around you with your heightened sense of observation. You will discover a new awareness of how people feel, and what eye contact is like. In a way, you will realise how blind you have been previously.

Mastering the Sense of Touch – Wind Element

As you awaken, instantly bring your focus to the sense of touch. Don't move at all, but just focus on what you can feel initially. Mentally scan through the whole of your body, taking note of your position and the sensation in each of your limbs. Note the feel of your bedclothes, your body heat and even the springs of the mattress – bring everything into your awareness. Keep your focus on the sense of touch, perhaps moving slightly as you explore each sensation. As you arise, vow to take this increased awareness into your everyday life.

As you go through your day you will notice how much touch is usually ignored. You may feel the clothing on your body or the glasses on your nose. Sensations that you normally ignore completely will now be in your awareness. You will feel the tension in your muscles and the movement in your digestive system. Notice the movement when you are on the train or driving your car. If you find your sense of touch is not responding as the others did, then take a few moments to consciously 'will' every muscle in your entire body to relax and calm.

Mastering the Sense of Hearing – Void Element

The sense of hearing is very important to the Ninja and should be developed to the highest degree possible. To do this you need, upon awakening, to move your focus to your hearing. Listen to whatever the noise in your environment is. It may be an alarm waking you up. You may be able to hear the noise of traffic or of bird song. Put your mind on the noises around you. Focus not just on the sounds you hear but on the detail of the sounds. So, for example, you may hear the noise of scraping and of footsteps and then of a lorry moving, which indicates that there is a refuse truck nearby. You may hear light running footsteps then a pause and some female voices and then more running, suggesting that a jogger stopped to talk to a friend. Bring this increased awareness into your daily life.

Continue your analysis of sound during the day and keep your focus on gaining extra information from it. Notice how heavy someone's steps are when walking to see their secretary, and how light they are when going to see their boss. Notice how different noises and types of music affect your body and your other senses. Make a note of how people's voice tones change depending on who they are talking to and when.

I started to practise the exercises. For me they were very emotive and seemed to be having more of a change on me internally that you would initially think. I believe this exercise, combined with continual analysis and application of elemental strategy in life, brought me to a brand-new height of awareness. However, I began to wonder about another sense – a sense the Ninja were legendary for – that of the sixth sense or 'danger sense'.

How to Sense Danger

With my new focus came a new awareness that I could see many things in To-Shin Do teachings that had been invisible to me before. For example, when we were practising techniques, I never realised that it is in fact always your turn. The whole system is set up so the attacker is learning to attack, while the defender learns to defend. It kept it realistic as a form of awareness training.

Awareness training I knew was legendary in Ninjutsu. I asked Stephen about this and he said that he could show me only what his instructor Masaaki Hatsumi had showed him when asked about the danger sense.

I expected another steep spiritual exercise, but instead the answer was rather interesting. He told me to make sure that whenever I practised, every strike I made at someone else had pure intention in it. I reflected on what he had said. By using intention I would learn to sense intention and hopefully my partner would reflect this nervous intention back at me with each strike. To feel it, to sense it and to have an instinct for it; this is a way in which a Ninja can defend himself against an unseen opponent.

Stephen explained that this was extremely important as one day I would have to take a test whereby a live blade would be held behind my head while I was blindfolded. I would have to sense the intention or *Sake* as it is called in Japan, as somebody lifted the sword high above my head and filled themselves with the most terrible rage and intent to kill. As they struck I would have to roll out of the way just in time, purely by sensing the danger. I took a deep breath.

In ancient Japan without this awareness you could get caught from behind, crept up on or poisoned. So this was something the Ninja had to develop a great deal in the past. Of course, this is also why we need to drill so many techniques with realism in the modern day, to develop this sixth sense for danger.

Over the next week, I paid attention to my sixth sense and my awareness of it began to grow. Through my sensory exercises, I started to see the world differently. I began to feel more aware and respond to things with greater ease; I truly had started to learn. But my greatest challenge was about to begin – that of learning to use the Wind element.

I particularly remember one lesson when Stephen Hayes walked in the room. It was a rare moment. He was about to teach the whole class. Before the class started, he walked to the front of the room and made a gesture.

He held his hand in a kind of pointing gesture – two fingers forward, two fingers back like a sword in his hand – and he then drew in front of him a grid and a series of symbols, muttering something under his breath. I felt a change in energy move across the whole room. I knew there was something called *Kuji kuri* or 'nine magical cuts'. Was he performing this sacred *Kuji kuri*? But, if so, why did the whole room change? It felt very interesting.

The lesson started with a meditation of purification. The meditation is as follows.

Imagine yourself as you sit there. Relax your breathing and imagine there is another figure, a figure that loves you – a divine aide who is there to do everything good for you and who pours cold cleansing water upon your head. As this water flows, it fills your entire being, churning and removing all evil and impurity.

I was finding it very hard to focus during this meditation. My legs were so tired. I sought to prove to Stephen Hayes that I had some skill in something, and meditation is an area that I had studied and practised for many years, but the pain was such that my breathing was deep and I was finding it hard just to hold on.

After the lesson, I explained the problem that I had had to Stephen who said that sometimes during meditation it can be good to have something to ignore. I started to apply this principle to my own meditation and it stands to be completely correct. It is almost like having a focus not to focus on.

It made me realise that much of Ninjutsu is about using whatever circumstance it is to your advantage. When I talked to Stephen, I asked him about the cuts. He explained to me that this was a special blessing. Not the mind cuts of legend, but one that really helps to bless the mood and leads to safe practice for everyone. That, then, was the change I had sensed. It seemed there was a lot more to this Ninja magic than I had first thought.

FU KUJI GOSHIN-GO (WIND ENERGY CHANNELLING SELF-PROTECTION METHOD)

The Secret of Focused Intention
To invoke the Wind state of consciousness, imagine yourself as a figure that represents the ability to disappear, confuse and misdirect. To summon the inner storm visualise an image that represents positive qualities of Air. Imagine how it would feel if you were that epitome of stealth and agility, moving faster than your opponent and confusing him with your outstanding abilities. You could imagine yourself as a natural phenomenon like a tornado or hurricane. If you feel a connection with animals you could imagine yourself as a hawk swooping from nowhere and flying away after each attack or, if you have ever experienced an angry goose spitting and attacking, you may see the Wind qualities in that animal.

The Secret of the Spoken Vow
The traditional way is to use a form of breathing associated with this element. To do this, inhale quickly and forcefully to the upper chest. Feel your lungs expand. Then exhale with a long steady breath. Imagine your breath is a gust of wind or a swelling vortex of force.

The Secret of Embodied Action
To trigger the Wind state of mind, form rings with the thumbs (Void element) and the pointer fingers (Wind element) of both hands. Entwine the two rings your fingers have formed and touch the tips of the other fingers together. Hold your hand in a praying position in front of your chest.

All three of the above should be performed simultaneously. Form your symbolic image of your goal in your mind's eye. Inhale using the Wind breath while forming the hand position. You need to use all three methods as a tool to reinforce your intent. Energetically will your adoption of the Wind mind state. Raise your joined hands up over your head, then pull them back to your chest. As you exhale, thrust your conjoined hands forward in front of your chest, inhale and return them to the position over your heart. With imagination, word and action in unity, set your resolve and invoke your inner Wind force.

Kusurifundo

At the Quest Center they practised using many different weapons: swords, knives, clubs and traditional weapons from Japan. Almost all of them were both for attack and self-defence.

There are many modern equivalents. One weapon, which I immediately fell in love with, was called the Kusurifundo. The Kusurifundo is a length of chain with a metal weight on either end.

In class we used a small piece of rope and knotted it on the end. It is easy to conceal: you can roll it up in your hands, attack and let it disappear. The positions that we used to fight with have it concealed from the beginning.

For me, it was the easiest and most tactical weapon for the modern day because a belt would serve just the same purpose. You can take your belt off and use it as a devastating weapon. You can wrap someone's wrists, tie them up and wait for the police to arrive. The Kusurifundo uses Wind footwork, and it was through the love of this weapon that I started to get the feel of this element.

Little Dog Appears

One evening I left the dojo talking to some of the younger black belts. We went to the local restaurant to have a Chinese meal with some of the other students. However, fate was to put another challenge in my way that evening.

The little dog that barks at the big dog was about to appear. One of the teenage students from the dojo had heard the story of my defeat at the hands of Stephen Hayes, and I was sitting there explaining to him how impressed I was and unable to believe how unskilled I was. I was telling him how great his master was. As we ended the meal, he asked me to list my previous martial arts qualifications, which I did. I saw a flash of realisation in his face. I didn't recognise it at the time, but I was soon to realise he had mentally made a calculation. He underestimated Master Hayes and thus saw my defeat at his hands as a sign of weakness.

As we left the building, there was a sudden change in his demeanour. He became aggressive and challenged me to fight. It was a set-up. He had deliberately asked me about my martial arts experience so that he could respond as a challenged male. As he stood there, many things ran through my mind.

Firstly, that one of the action codes – the code of conduct, the To-Shin Do – was never to attack or use violence unnecessarily, avoiding violence whenever you can. I also thought about what Master Norris had said about the little dog barking.

I looked at this young lad, and though he had had a great teacher, the 17-year-old boy had no idea what kind of fighting experience I had had. The pure level of nasty intense violence that I had experienced under the tuition of Karl and Shaun left me in a very good situation to hurt him very badly. There was a brick lying on the wall next to me. I could see his legs move as the adrenalin surged through his body.

I wondered if it was a test, if Stephen Hayes or one of the other black belts had put him up to this. More likely fate had a hand in this test. So what was I going to do? All the other students were gathered round, waiting to see what was going to happen.

So I just walked away. I walked away from the situation, even though part of me wanted to fight. But what would I gain by proving that I had not learned anything?

As I got back to my hotel, I felt upset. I had really trusted him and been open with my emotions. Then another emotion stirred inside, another rage – I was angry with Stephen Hayes!

I began to realise that many of Stephen's critics had arrived at this stage emotionally before. They had seen how brilliant he was. They had seen his skills. They had realised that it would be extremely hard for them to match him. This jealousy had turned to hatred and they had never got over it. It is hard, if your centre of self-esteem is based on an art, when you meet someone who is obviously better. I, however, was going to conquer my internal demons so that I could learn from this master – so that I could learn the lessons of this true American Ninja. I was not going to make the mistakes others did in letting my ego control my actions or of not recognising how rare and special his teachings were.

Making Friends with Death

There is something about Stephen Hayes I found very hard to deal with. It took me a long time to put my finger on it. It was only during my final week in Dayton that it finally dawned on me.

It was something about his inner self. Stephen wasn't attached to things. He was like a void. The Stephen Hayes that was born had disappeared a long time ago.

The new enlightened Stephen, with balanced elements, didn't respond to any of my games or engage with things outside his focus. He just had a loving detachment, something that I started to appreciate far more when I asked him about the mysterious bone skull beads both he and some of the senior black belts wore on their wrists.

Stephen showed me the bracelet on his wrist. I had seen similar bracelets on James Norris. Both parties told me that this had been a gift from a friend; I suspect that this was the Dalai Lama. The skulls were smiling and laughing.

"These are our reminder beads. We wear them to remind us of death, dealing with death, and the fear of the inevitability of death. This a very important question, not just from a philosophical world view but also from a Ninja warrior point of view.

"The beads literally are a piece of death, made from the bones of a dead animal, reminding you that one day that will be you and that knowledge makes you better and improves you.

"You notice that the skulls on these beads are depicted smiling and laughing. To begin with, the laughing, teasing skulls are saying to you: 'When's it going to come? When are you going to die?' This reminds you that it could happen at any moment – death is laughing at you.

"Now this all sounds really scary but it's really rather good. You see, because they remind you, they bring an awareness of death and make you remember how important it is to do what you need to do while you're still alive.

"They remind you of the urgency of the work, the urgency in your life to make every moment count, and because you make every moment count, because you focus on being the most noble, dignified and positive influence you can be on the world, death starts to become your friend. And because it becomes your friend, soon when you look at the skulls, they're smiling because they're your friends, not because they are laughing."

The Warrior's Journey

Stephen explained that what I had gone through was traditional. The warrior's journey is a well-known part of Japanese martial arts. It is by travelling that you really get to know yourself. When you get out of your normal environment you lose three important things; your Name, your Elements, and the Void.

The Name represents your reputation. In your normal environment people know who you are, your history and your past achievements. None of these things can accompany you on your travels, so people judge you afresh – how you are presently – without knowing the past. This, for the spiritual warrior, shows him the truth about himself – his present self. It is rather like a famous novelist publishing his work under a different name to see if it is skill or reputation that has the effect.

The Elements represent the way you cope with situations. This can be extremely telling because when we are in one environment for a certain time, interacting with the same events and the same people, we tend to respond habitually in a certain way. When we are put into different situations with different people, but with no support mechanisms, sometimes our strategies don't work and we have to learn to adapt. Once again, this can lead to an understanding of ourselves and how we come across to others. Most importantly it helps us learn to be more flexible and adaptable.

Finally, the Void. This represents our illusions about how things work. When we move into different environments, we sometimes discover that things we thought were universal are not so. Different societies have different taboos, different cultures and different ways of doing things. Sometimes we see something so differently that we are forced to change our underlying beliefs and misconceptions.

How to Fight Like the Wind

My body can do all the movements, but without that effortless feeling it is just not effective. It's hard to describe, but when you really achieve the state of mind it's almost like the combat is beneath you. It's like a pacifistic form of fighting – you float above such things.

The whole mechanics of the Wind element are based on a turning motion. This starts with *Hira no Kamae* which makes it extremely easy to be evasive and dodge with a pivot on one leg or the other. To fight like the Wind, you need to make your evasive movements part of your attack. You have to learn to spin, be quick, responsive, evasive and unpredictable.

This, of all the elemental strategies, is the hardest to achieve, and when you see someone using this fighting method, it is truly awesome.

Your opponent feels as if you have disappeared, like you are always just out of range, and you get a tremendous amount of force behind your strikes using this method. Like the Wind, your opponent is buffeted, blown from one side to another – confused, whipped, hurt in one whole motion. To be like the Wind you need to be quick, responsive and accurate. You are so close to the person that they can't hurt you. When you get Wind right, everything you do feels effortless and easy, your movements are light and nimble. The Wind state of mind is a difficult one to achieve, one that in Dayton I only fully touched on now and again.

Elemental Enlightenment

At the beginning of the month I asked James Norris how to understand elements. He told me that by using them I would truly learn to understand them. I had meditated on them, studied and contemplated everything I had read. I discovered that the traditional Ninja teaching classified everything using the elements and that this knowledge could be used not just to decide on your own strategy but also to understand your opponent's needs and weaknesses.

On the final day, in the morning, I had an enlightenment experience; something inside me had changed. My strategic ability expanded, my pride was gone and I had gained flexibility. I felt like I could see the world in a different way. I could see the whole world as a manifestation of the elements.

The Five Elemental Manifestations

Chi – Earth – a solid state, a natural posture
Sui – Water – a liquid state, a defensive posture
Ka – Fire – an energy-releasing state, an offensive posture
Fu – Wind – a gaseous state, a receiving posture
Ku – Void – subatomic energy, potential, the substance from which things take form.

I felt like somehow the vision of these five elements had opened up a different consciousness: an ability to see the big picture, to see the forces at work and an ability to think through any circumstance strategically.

Master Hayes had taught me about the emotions and how they relate to the elements. I realised that this had given me an ability to understand the emotions and thus use them in others. My own vision of the needs of others opened up before me. It was as if suddenly I could understand the motives behind the actions of myself and everyone else. It was like seeing the truth behind the illusion for the first time.

For me Ninjutsu was increasingly becoming the art of getting what you want. I had let go of the childish image of the Ninja as a silent assassin and realised the Ninja was a person who would be whatever was effective to achieve his goals. A lot of getting what you want is about making people do what you want. To do this you need to understand what people want. Through my contemplation and study, my own personal vision of these needs started to manifest itself. But in the end, Stephen was absolutely correct. I had been so focused in the elements and on using the strategies, both in the dojo and in the real world, that a profound change had come over me.

The Five Needs
The Ninja was also able to exploit the needs of an adversary. In doing so, it was possible to manipulate events and have debts repaid. The Ninja could then be at the centre of activity yet remain hidden.

It is worth noting here that the traditional sets of elemental needs do vary.

• Purpose

Corresponding to the Void or Spirit element. This is the highest possible motive for a person. Genuine purpose, however, is truly very rare. Most people's actions are completely driven by one of the other motives/elements below. However, we tend to hide our motives from ourselves and others on purpose.

• Power

Corresponding to the Fire element. The urge to be in control and to be able to dictate what happens in the world around us dictates so many people's actions. It is why we push ourselves and fight hard for things.

• Social Status

Corresponding to the verbal, social Wind element. Wanting to look good in front of others and achieve high status in the pack. It is a powerful motivator.

• Sex/Need for love

Corresponding to the emotional Water element. This controls the sexual centre and is also a powerful motivator. It drives us hard to win friends and to put ourselves into a position in which people want us.

• Security

Corresponding to the Earth element. Ultimate fear is the motivator for security. This is also what is behind much of the motivation for possessions or money, wanting to protect ourselves against the world.

In life, we all like to pretend we are moved primarily by the Spirit or Void element. That is to say, we always claim that we are acting for a purpose, for a higher and nobler cause.

But the truth is there are four other elements which are more likely to be controlling our decisions. Earth, for example, would be about material possessions or the security that they bring. Water would be more about sexuality or the fulfilment of our emotions. Fire would be about ambition and power. And wind would be about social status and standing.

These emotions, these aspects of our personality, are those that control us. By using these and understanding the elements, we can strategically make people do what we want. Ninjutsu is about achieving this goal.

To be able to do this, we first need to understand ourselves, to eliminate these emotions and ways of being. So we need to learn to be honest about what we want. Only then can we start to deceive, control and manipulate others. Of course, these are tools that we all use for the higher good.

Here is an example of how this philosophy could be applied.

Imagine you are in 7th-century Japan. You want to sell a piece of land to a nearby Buddhist monastery. When you approach the monk or abbot in charge, you are probably tempted to use Buddhism and purpose as the means to convince him.

Now Ninjutsu teaches that although people would pretend that purpose is their ultimate motivation, it is probably better for you to allow him to choose the other emotions but letting them hide within purpose. You could say to him, "Listen, I really want to sell you this land and I think it would be very good for your monastery and Buddhism. But I want you to be aware that we have had other offers, including one from a western Christian missionary who wants to buy the land to build a church here."

Now this, on the Earth level, would make him fearful and appeal to his sense of fear of rival religions and alien things. This would allow him to believe he was purchasing the land out of the Buddhist noble doctrine. But in fact he is fearful of Christians moving in.

If Earth doesn't work, perhaps he is a Water element kind of person. Perhaps you could appeal to something sexual. Of course, this is a monk who shouldn't have any of these feelings, but when you start to work with the elements you become rather cynical and see the true motives behind people's action. So you could say to him something like this: "Perhaps it's about time that there was a convent here, a Buddhist convent that perhaps could work in association with your monastery." Now this, on a very subconscious base level, may well appear to the abbot to be a possibility, as having close interaction with females is essentially a sublimation of his sexual urge. This could persuade him to purchase the land.

Or you could use Fire as a strategy and say to him, "Think of the power, think of the influence you could have. Maybe you need your own special school, maybe you need to be promoted as the head of a new monastery. Perhaps with this land you could increase your influence." This would appeal to him if he was Fire personality.

If he was a Wind personality you could say to him, "Think of the influence, think of the fame. You're such a good teacher that it's your duty to put yourself forward with this. It's your duty to have a big stage, a large school to spread Buddhism. It's not for you, not for your own fame, not for your own ego, but because you have a duty, with the kind of skill that you have as a teacher, to do this for others."

Through this elemental enlightenment, I began to know almost intuitively what kind of elemental person I was talking to. I found myself switching elemental strategy very easily. I also discovered my own real motives. I no longer hid them and lied to myself. Everything looked bigger and clearer to me, as if a divine vision of the world had opened up. I felt empowered; I felt stronger.

I had gained some tools. This whole elemental outlook was the most important skill I have ever learned in my life. And since then, I have used the elements to gain great success in every single area of my life. This has given me a greater insight into the small world inside me and into the big world around me.

The elements had become part of me and my way of working. Every single day I was improving. In a sense, I felt I had learned the true essence of To-Shin Do – something more valuable than anything I could have purchased. I also started to see the weaknesses these needs give us.

The Five Weaknesses
Again, these are my personal set; traditional ones may vary.
• Confusion
• Anger/ambition
• Vanity
• Sympathy
• Fear

These, of course, are connected with the person's needs. It is the emotion that helps to control the person.

Someone looking for purpose shows confusion; a person looking for power shows anger and ambition (ambition is the urge to make things how you want them and anger is the same but amplified); someone looking for social status shows vanity; the urge for love shows as sympathy; and the urge for security manifests from fear. My vision of the elements was starting to develop slightly differently from others' and indeed from what I had initially been taught. This didn't worry me, as to me this showed how genuine and powerful what had happened was. And, of course, it was completely in keeping with To-Shin Do tradition to grab the ball and run with it. But all this elemental experience had got me suspicious. I wondered if there was something that Stephen Hayes was keeping secret from the world.

Tulku – The Secret Art

It seemed to me a bit suspicious that Stephen had spent so many years guarding the Dalai Lama and I knew that he had been studying the secret of Tibetan Buddhism while he was there. I, however, had another suspicion. There is a legendary martial art of Tibet, so mysterious that we don't actually know if it is real or not.

It is called the *Tulku*. The idea is that all elements make a similar roar or noise to the spinning prayer wheel when they are powerfully applied – the roar of a fire, of a hurricane, of a rock slide or a waterfall. Somewhere in Tibet there was a martial art that teaches you to use the elements. It was interesting that Stephen should have chosen that for his next destination after his Ninja studies in Japan.

Could it be that he went there to learn a martial art that would be so in line with Ninjutsu that part of me suspected that it was the original source of the art?

The Tibetan martial art, *Tulku*, is only just spoken of, whispered almost, as if it can't exist and is kept secret from everyone in the world. The Dalai Lama, however, must have disciples that know it.

It must be part of the teachings. Stephen had spent so much time in the Himalayas with these masters; it would be unbelievable that he wouldn't even have sought out this art based on the same elements as Ninjutsu. But how to find out?

The lesson was starting: it was a form of contemplation. In this exercise, you go back through your day and look at the things you have done and find one little thing that you could have done better. And then in your mind, you adjust how you would have done it. It is a form of awareness training, leading to continual self-improvement.

After the lesson, I just asked Stephen straight, "When you were in Tibet, did you learn the *Tulku*?" It was the first time I had ever seen him respond with some form of surprise. I think he was taken aback by the idea that I even knew it existed. He was evasive.

"These are things that people do talk about sometimes in Tibet; it's only mentioned occasionally."

I knew at that precise moment that he had. That not only had this man learned from the last living Ninja, but some of the things in the To-Shin Do syllabus were part of this sacred Tibetan martial art, and that he had expanded the techniques available using it, something that I suspect he would never talk about or admit to in his lifetime.

As I left the Quest Center I felt great sadness. I had found a group of people with the same purpose as me. They were on the path of self-improvement and through self-development they were improving the world around them for others. But I was inspired! Karl and Shaun had been wrong about Ninja classes. It was time for me to put my head down and actually apply what I had learned.

CHAPTER FIVE

A TIME IN THE DESERT

Yamabushi Training

As soon as I got back to England I continued my elemental training. I knew that much of the knowledge of the elements in Ninjutsu came from the teaching of the legendary mountain mystics of Japan known as the Yamabushi. Yamabushi means 'mountain dwellers' and these mystical enigmas were known for their following of a path known as Shugendō which means 'attaining magical powers through hardship'. So linked with the Ninja were these mysterious figures that in some ancient texts the words are used synonymously. I started to read everything I could about the Yamabushi and their skills. I discovered that the lesson of facing the elements came directly from this path. The Yamabushi use many creative and varying methods to start to face the elements. Stephen Hayes' advanced students practice this kind of training in their spare time. Since my time visiting Dayton I had been informed that a waterfall and various other places needed for Yamabushi trials were being built on Stephen's private land for his advanced students to test their abilities. I, however, had learned not to rely on anyone else. So it was natural for me to face the elements alone. These trials are not a one-off event but an ongoing training method. From the Ninja point of view we are constantly being tested by the elements in life. These exercises help us master our inner elements so as to gain self-mastery.

The Trial of Earth

The first test for the Ninja would be the trial of Earth. The Yamabushi simply spent a day and a night in a cave. Sometimes the cave was so high up a cliff face that they had to wait for their fellow Bushi to come with ropes to fetch them. On other occasions they would have a boulder rolled in front of the cave entrance. The important thing about this trial, of course, is that the practitioner has to be still and in that stillness face himself. I explored the possibility of a cave, but almost all caves in England are on the coast and fill with water at night. So instead I chose a rock in the wilderness and simply decided to sit on it.

Far away from anyone else in the world, the Earth trial seemed very easy. There was no audience and my sole aim was one of self-development. It was a pleasant, natural setting and, after all, I was used to the dark from my training with Karl and Shaun. However, without a phone and with no way of telling the time, my mood started to change. I began to get an irresistible urge to move.

As time passed, my body started to complain. Sometimes it would be like it was trying to stand up on its own, and only through great will would I be able to keep it stationary. As darkness fell, it started to get very cold and damp. Why the hell didn't I bring a cushion? I was getting hungry and lonely. I thought of the people I loved. I started to wonder what the purpose of all this was. My mind started to construct reasons to give up and go home: I had a car under a mile away, I could sleep there. No one would know. My back was killing me. Anyway I could always come back and try again with a cushion.

The struggle between me and the Earth element was on and it was starting to win. I tried slowing my breathing to calm myself but the discomfort had become pain. Then it came to me – I would not simply sit and fight the element, I would embrace it. I would become at one with the stone beneath me. It didn't need anyone else. I never cried or became uncomfortable. I would move myself in harmony with it, so I performed my Earth element *Kuji* (as pictured) and summoned up the Earth state of mind. It worked. The whole experience started to be a pleasant one: a night to watch the animals pass by and be at one with the stars. This feeling would last for a while, perhaps half an hour, and then I would have to repeat the process, but each time it got a bit easier. The next day I was exhausted as I dropped off my rock tired by the cold and by the fear of the dark that seemed to kick in with the inaction. I had not moved from that rock for exactly twenty-four hours. The Earth element had not defeated me and I had found something of my inner Earth inside. *(See fig.42)*

The Trial of Water

This is the most famous of all Yamabushi trials and the one most associated with the Ninja. It took me a while to realise why, but in Japanese legend and in modern fiction you become a Ninja through waterfall training. I also knew this was part of the training of Takamatsu Sensei, the teacher of Masaaki Hatsumi, and that the black belts under Stephen Hayes also valued it as a tool of self-improvement. I had read of and seen pictures of the Yamabushi practising under waterfalls during the winter when all around them is frozen. In England we have quite a few waterfalls, but those in Wales offer an abundance, with varying powers and forces. When I arrived at my chosen one, the Welsh name of which translates as 'snow falls', I realised I may have bitten off more than I could chew. The force with which the water came down was unbelievable. I knew that this kind of training was dangerous and that Takamatsu had passed out and floated down the river at one point. The water did look white as snow and the roar was monumental. It took a lot of guts to get near to it. As I waded up to the waterfall my body tensed with the cold. Wales is not the best place in the world for outdoor swimming in winter!

I stood in front of the waterfall and prepared myself mentally. It represented everything negative that stands in my way, everything that pushes me away from my spiritual callings and from living my life how I want to live it. I would not be moved, I would stay in the flow; the Water element would not defeat me. Remembering the trial of Earth, I performed my water *Kuji* and stepped into the waterfall.

The first thing that hit me was the coldness, and then the pressure. A thousand hands were slapping my head and back at every moment and I had to sit down as my legs started to give way. I kept performing my water *Kuji* as the cold turned to pain. My eyes stung and the force of the water blasted my contact lenses from them. Everything hurt and the whole of my being called out for me to stand up and get out of the water. I found myself counting the movements of my arms as I performed the water *Kuji*. I tried to become part of the waterfall. I don't know why, but I opened my eyes and right before me formed a rainbow. At that moment there was a moment of calm realisation – the Ninja is *he who endures*. That's why to the Japanese this training obviously makes you a Ninja because you learn to endure in the waterfall! My enduring, however, was over. I was starting to feel like I would pass out and float down the river.

I lay on the rocks, too tired and cold to move. I had overcome the waterfall! *(See fig.43)*

Fig.42   *Fig.43*

The Trial of Fire

The Yamabushi themselves light hot fires in a circle and sit in the centre to resist the heat. They also make long fires and run through the flames. I, however, when contemplating my trial, had a sudden inspiration: I would retreat to the desert and face the sun, a common method of mystical challenge. I found a place to stay in rural Egypt and started a daily practice in the hottest place on earth.

The first day was the worst. I had been driven to the desert away from shelter and asked the driver to come back in two hours. This time I did bring a meditation cushion. It didn't help. I closed my eyes and focused on my breathing. I expected it to be hot – I had been to Egypt before – but I soon realised that there is a big difference between the temperature in Luxor and that of the Sahara!

Just as in the Earth trial and that of Water, the first emotion I felt was that of wanting to move. The initial heat of my legs on the sand made me jump, but as I settled down I began to realise why it was so tremendously hot in the first place. The sun beat down on me relentlessly. I felt like an ant being burned by a magnifying glass. I wanted to flee but had nowhere to go. Unlike at the waterfall, I couldn't just back out. I tried to move position, but nothing took the heat away. I was feeling the connection and intensity of the Fire element at first hand. This, I thought, was how the opponent should feel when I use the Fire element against him. For the first time in my trials I started to panic. How bad would I burn? What if I passed out? What if my driver didn't come back or couldn't find the obscure area he had left me in? Was I going to die? Should I start walking to somewhere now? They say 'mad dogs and Englishmen go out in the midday sun', but even a rabid dog would have instinctively hidden from this heat!

I knew I had to get a hold of myself. I had stood up without thinking. I looked at my watch. I had been there only 20 minutes. I sat down with a firm determination. I knew that no matter how impossible it seemed, I would have to use the same approach, to use the Fire *Kuji* and be in harmony with the Fire element. I had to fight fire by being fire. I started my practice and tried to focus on the heat as if it was a positive thing, to focus on my fear as if it was excitement. I decided to count a hundred repetitions of Fire breaths and just keep going. I continued and things started to get very dreamy through heat and hyperventilation. Something started to shift within me. I raised my determination to a fierce level; I was not going to be moved internally or externally. I was going to sit calmly until my car arrived. The heat from the sun seemed to intensify, to challenge my willpower, so I increased my inner intensity to keep going. I would be more Fire than the sun. I felt a spark of anger inside and then I had it. The burning pain just focused me. I opened my eyes and the heatwave from the desert reminded me of the waterfall. I knew I had defeated the Fire element. *(See fig.44)*

The Trial of Wind

The traditional trial as practised by the Yamabushi is to hang upside down off a cliff from a rope while confessing your sins or to sit on the very edge of a sheer drop and face the fear of death. I chose the second of the two and started searching for a cliff. It was not long before I found the perfect place on the coast that had a peak overlooking a deadly drop onto rocks and the sea below.

To get there I had to negotiate a lot of crumbling sandstone, climb over barbed-wire and walk through many metres of thorns. By the time I got there I was already cut, tired and bruised. I looked at the peak and, to my horror, it was at the end of a length of rock thinner than my shoulder width. I would have to crawl. The wind was up and I started to wonder if I would be blown to my death. I began to crawl along the edge. Ouch! It was covered in twigs of long dead thorns, which didn't add to my confidence. As I got near my target I started to feel fear rising. Would the sandstone hold me? The peak I was about to sit on was small and I weighed rather a lot. Was there going to be a newspaper article about my death by misadventure?

I got there and sat down. I could see for ever. The height made me feel slightly dizzy. The wind was pleasant which was fine at first, but then it began to buffet me. I was terrified not just of the wind but of the terror that it invoked. I had to keep my head. If fear overcame me, I might do something drastic to escape and lose my co-ordination. The wind buffeted me again, this time from a different direction. It was very scary not knowing which direction I was going to be pushed next and I was afraid to over-adjust. Sometimes if I pushed back against the wind, when it stopped I would suddenly be off balance. I had a few nasty moments like that. I started my air *Kuji*. It was nerve-racking for it involved moving my hands above my head, but I carried on and as I continued I began to realise that the wind was nowhere near as strong as I thought. It would never harm me. When was the last time you saw someone blown over by the wind? Something about the movement made it less noticeable and I was more stable. A lovely calmness over came me. This calmness seemed beyond worldly things up there on the cliff. Then the feeling scared me; it made me worry I might become over-confident and fall. This calm/terrified fluctuation continued for a while until I found a happy medium – alert but not over-emotional. I could have stayed there all day. I had defeated the wind element. Little did I know that I had a final, even more terrible, elemental trial ahead – that of the Void. *(See fig.45)*

I had finished my elemental trials and resumed my nightly stealth training. Every day I would have new insights into the Ninja mindset. I was beginning to see the truth, to see how people really worked, what they thought, and indeed my true goals in life were coming into focus. I thirsted for the support of like-minded people; I needed people to practise with and to learn from. Karl and Shaun had discouraged me from attending classes, but I had learned so much from my time in Dayton that I now knew their advice to be wrong. I knew almost all the classes in Britain were run directly under the dojo of the Ninja Grand Master Masaaki Hatsumi. He called his group of martial art schools Bujinkan – meaning 'heavenly warrior hall'. While I was away on a business trip, I decided to visit a class based in Britain.

The Trial of Void

As soon as I entered the room I was aware of a different feel to the whole class. It was far more relaxed. Everyone was wearing green belts and talking. I talked to the head instructor, explaining who I was, where I had trained and what my aims were.

The instructor was horrified by what I said and spent the next 30 minutes explaining how stupid and incorrect all the teachings of Stephen Hayes were, attacking his character and dismissing all 'that spiritual nonsense'. He then went on to explain that his club was independent and how incorrect the approach of the Ninja Grand Master Hatsumi was. I stood in stunned silence. As the class started, my shock turned to horror.

The whole class was based on rules: keeping the feet exactly in line, making sure the shoulder aligns exactly with the shoulder, and repeating

Fig.44   *Fig.45*

the same movement again and again. At one point I was told by an instructor that my Tabi boots were holding me back. I needed to wear special indoor Tabi or it would be impossible for me to perform the movements correctly. I couldn't believe it. I was being taught a martial art that would only work on a flat floor with special leather-soled shoes. What the hell was I doing?

If it didn't work, if it wasn't practical, no matter who it was, no matter where they said they trained or what qualifications they said they had, I had to reject what they were teaching. I realised at that time that something had happened to Ninjutsu somewhere. Good technique was now judged by a set of rigid rules and not by its effectiveness.

I had felt the lightning bolt of truth and purpose. They had to work. Ninjutsu was the art of survival. Ninjutsu was the art of power and winning. Nothing else was important.

Every movement was like a bizarre parody of the arts I was taught in Dayton, jerky and inefficient and so overwhelmingly and obviously impractical that I found it hard to take seriously – a problem that, in the weeks to follow, I discovered was endemic. Over the next few weeks I visited every class my work allowed me as I travelled around the country.

On my travels I discovered a great variation in opinions. Each instructor I visited was sure he knew the genuine way of doing things. I got to see the massive variation in what was being taught in dojos. I also discovered that almost two out of three classes were part of renegade breakaway groups. In fact it seemed to me that for every two classes that were following Hatsumi Sensei's regimes there were another six who had become independent or joined some other group.

Ironically the best class I found was close to home. The instructor really was genuine in his dedication to the art. I respected his position. His view of teaching was like a meditation on the technique and was very calming and perfectionist. But our views of the art differed. I was restless and focused on gaining power and self-discovery, so after a couple of months I moved on.

As I toured the country I found that what the classes all had in common was that they seemed tense, rigid and, most of all, impractical. Nothing flowed; it was all jerky and uncomfortable. Many of the people I talked to were very disrespectful about Stephen Hayes. Indeed, I had to endure terrible insults against him and some of his students from people who didn't have an eighth of his skill, talent or understanding of the art.

Ninja Vs Ninja

One class I attended in the north of England had a very aggressive instructor. He held a Fifth Dan in the art, but was instantly upset at the mention of Stephen Hayes and became really nasty when I started to ask questions. At the end of the class he took me to one side to 'show' me some moves. He was pushing me about and basically bullying me. He asked about my martial arts history and I told him. I had just fallen for the same old trick.

"So you're a tough guy, yeah? Think you're a hard nut?"

It reminded me of Shane Stevens when he was in 'tough guy' role-playing mode.

I am unsure if he went to grab or punch me, but whatever he did I grabbed his arm and put him in my trademark arm bar. His arm did not melt like Hayes' but locked out painfully. He struggled like a man possessed, leaping around the dojo like a frog, dragging me all over the place. He must have been in the most terrible pain. Somehow in all the chaos he smashed his own face on the floor and a flow of crimson blood covered the mats. By now the receptionist of the sports centre had appeared along with a couple. I let go of the instructor's arm. He reeled back in pain, trying to bend it. I will never forget the look of concern on the receptionist's face as I paid for my class and left. Whenever two people fight, the results are always negative. At that point I vowed never again to get involved in such macho rubbish.

Will the Real Stephen K. Hayes Please Stand Up?

There is a type of instructor like the one above who is full of resentment and bitter jealousy. It is rather strange but they despise Stephen Hayes and attempt to destroy him by being as like him as possible. They grow a beard, get the clothes and talk nastily in corners. I call these people Hayz-a-bes and they are the most dangerous of instructors. I met a fair few of them – oozing half-venom, half-ignorance. I remember talking to a very famous American Hayz-a-be of great rank and fame who was criticising the verbal commands used as part of To-Shin Do training.

"'Stop! Stop! Stay back!' That's not very silent or Ninja. Whoever heard of a Ninja attacking while making noise?" he said, chuckling to himself.

He should have been laughing *at* himself. The man had no idea what it was to be a Ninja. No idea that being a Ninja is about being adaptable and doing whatever makes you win. Did he think a Ninja walked down the street in his black suit? Did he think that you would be silent while posing as someone else? Who is the new silent black-clad cleaner silently dusting the castle?

This kind of brainless illogical criticism filled the classes I went to and also fills the internet. I remember one day someone talking about a television programme that Stephen Hayes was in. "Yeah, he is a good fighter and can do dangerous things, but his technique is crap."

I felt like asking, "What is technique for?" It was like saying that Leonardo da Vinci was very good, but I don't like the way he holds his brush!

I started to wonder if the main problem Stephen had was not being Japanese. However, even Japanese masters were not beyond criticism. I heard people telling me that their master in Ireland was the only person teaching the true arts and that Hatsumi no longer taught the truth.

My head was in a swirl with all this negativity and continual dramatic contradictions about what I should do. I became negative about my practice. No one was like me. No one understood me. I was living in a world where everything I did was strange. How strange to think that in these Ninja classes, my practising of throwing stars, stealth and *Kuji-in* was laughable. They saw me as a weirdo. Where were the real Ninja?

I remember one day returning home and talking to my wife. I was distraught.

"I don't understand; as a Ninja we are meant to be at one with Nature. The whole point is that if you are at one with Nature, no one can defeat you. All our movements then must be natural, relaxed and effective."

My wife responded, "Perhaps Ninjutsu is not something anyone can grasp; perhaps it takes a rare individual to really get it."

I paused in reflection.

"Perhaps Stephen Hayes is the only westerner to really get it?" she added.

That made me think she was almost right. I thought about Karl and Shaun, Stephen Hayes and James Norris. It seemed to me that they all had one thing in common: they fully embraced the art with the whole of their beings and wanted to learn all aspects of it. Many of the other teachers I had met limited what they learned to the safe, normal martial arts class and self-defence. There must be other people in England who had also 'got it', but with so many conflicting opinions and with everyone accusing Hayes of making up what he was taught, I didn't have the time or the ability to discover the truth.

But the sheer number of people I was visiting, some of whom had even trained in Japan yet knew nothing of the elements, who viewed *Kuji-in* and meditation as mere superstition, was overwhelming.

I started to wonder who was telling the truth. Had Stephen brought all this stuff in from Tibet? Was the real Ninjutsu spiritless? Was it just simply a way to play tricks on the gullible? But the lessons I had learned were so valuable that I couldn't believe them to be from any other tradition. They just felt so right.

Every time I attended a class, my spirit was being broken. I didn't want to be practising some form of Tai Chi, trying to get my movements specific to a rule. I wanted to learn to fight. I wanted to learn something that changed me inside. I wanted to be challenged in a different way, in a higher way.

I looked at the skull beads on my wrist. It was time to find the truth. I couldn't waste any more time with lessons that weren't in line with my spirit and my way of doing things. They didn't seem genuine, productive or useful.

They were lessons that didn't teach stealth, didn't teach spiritual matters, didn't teach meditation and didn't teach any form of fighting, which I felt would work in the modern, real world. Some of the movements seemed so ridiculous that they could have been made up just to see if anyone would believe them. I was distraught. Why would Grand Master Hatsumi allow this to happen?

Proof of the Art's Effectiveness

I was walking through south London early one morning, having attended a talk the previous evening. I was still half asleep and the cold London breeze blew rubbish along the street. Suddenly there was a wrench on my right arm and I turned to see what was happening. One of two black teenagers was trying to snatch my bag. He had attempted to snatch and run, but on feeling the tug I had naturally sunk into a low stance and gripped hard. This had tugged him back and almost thrown him off his feet. A sense of shock and detachment hit me. I couldn't believe it was really happening. However, my body was already in action. Wham! My left hand hit his wrist with a hammer fist. "Stop! Stop! Stay back!" I heard myself saying. With each phrase I ended with a punch to the mugger's face. There was a terrible crunch as his nose squashed under my fist.

There was a pause. Now he was the one that didn't believe what was happening.

His friend behind him took a step forward and this woke me from my temporary daze. This could be a really nasty fight. There were two of them; they could be armed! I took a step to the side so that one youth shielded me from the other. I jumped as their bodies lurched into action. They ran off without saying a word.

I had just performed a textbook To-Shin Do defence against a wrist grab from behind. All the practice had programmed the prefect response.

The pivot, the hammer fists, the attacker's wrist and the verbal distractions; everything flowed perfectly. I was living proof of the practical effectiveness of the To-Shin Do system, but was it genuine and authentic?

The Gordian Knot

In Greek legend, the Gordian knot was the name given to an intricate knot used by Gordius to secure his ox cart. Gordius, who was a poor peasant, arrived with his wife in a public square of Phrygia in his cart. An oracle had informed the populace that their future king would come riding in a wagon. Seeing Gordius, the people made him king. In gratitude, Gordius dedicated his ox cart to Zeus, tying it up with a peculiar knot. An oracle foretold that he who untied the knot would rule all of Asia. Many people tried to undo the knot, but all to no avail.

In 333BC Alexander the Great had invaded Asia Minor and arrived in the central mountains at the town of Gordium. He was 23 years of age. Undefeated, but without a decisive victory either, he was in need of an omen to prove to his troops and his enemies that the outcome of his mission – to conquer the known world – was possible.

In Gordium, by the Temple of the Zeus Basilica, was the ox cart, which had been put there by the King of Phrygia over 100 years before. The staves of the cart were tied together in a complex knot with the ends tucked away inside.

Having arrived at Gordium it was inconceivable that the young, impetuous king would not tackle the legendary Gordian knot. Alexander climbed the hill and approached the cart as a crowd of curious Macedonians and Phrygians gathered around. They watched intently as he struggled with the knot, becoming increasingly frustrated.

Alexander drew his sword and in one powerful stroke severed the knot!

The world of Ninjutsu is just like the Gordian knot – confused and intricate. Hundreds of schools and authorities all claim to know the truth. Bujinkan, Genbukan, Tenshin Shōden Katori Shintō-ry , To-Shin Do, Genbukan, Robert Bussey's American Ninjutsu, Fuma Ryu, Jinenkan – the list is endless.

All masters claim to be teaching the truth, all professing to have the genuine teachings. But what is the truth? Many have tried to 'cut the knot'. I had to find a way to take a sword and cut deep into the heart of the knot to reveal the truth.

CHAPTER SIX

JOURNEY TO THE EAST

Boarding the plane, I noticed that most of the passengers were Japanese. It seems that the Japanese have a bigger sense of adventure than westerners. More of them were returning to their native country than there were westerners travelling to the Land of the Rising Sun. I wanted to connect with them. I wanted to reach Japan somehow through the passengers on the plane. I think I felt it would ease my nerves if I was to learn something about life in Japan, but I soon discovered that I was the only English-speaking person within direct conversational range.

As the flight took off, I pondered on my strategy. I had trained with professional thieves and thugs. I had trained with Masaaki Hatsumi's first American student, Stephen K. Hayes, and now I was flying to Tokyo, hurling myself into the void without any form of introduction or response from my letter to the Ninja Grand Master. I was to travel directly to his dojo in Noda city to learn the teachings directly from the source.

I knew my strategy would have to be different from that employed with an American. If Americans didn't respond very well to my boasting and arrogant ways, in Japan the same actions would be disastrous. I had bought a green belt, knowing that students of the Bujinkan School up to a greater black belt wore only a green belt, so I would fit in.

I bought indoor Tabi boots, the Ninja footwear, so that I would be able to show that I was a dedicated student, and I had read the handbook on travelling to Japan. I decided right then and there to use an opposite strategy. I would be the most traditionally respectful and courteous student I could be. I would learn as much Japanese as I could to make sure that in the dojo I came across as a dedicated student, and I would listen to and memorise everything that I was told and shown.

As I turned to collect my Japanese meal, I noticed that some of the Japanese around me had put on surgical masks. Did it smell in the aircraft? Did they think that someone was contagious? It seemed rather sinister. Should I put my shoes back on?

I can never sleep on long-haul flights, and this was no exception. So I spent my time studying the works of Masaaki Hatsumi. His words were poetic and symbolic and amazingly wise, and I could tell he was an enlightened man. But I could also just as well tell that many of his words were lost in translation, both of language and culture.

As we landed in Tokyo after 13 hours of flight, I hadn't had a moment of sleep. Tokyo was just starting to get going, and I knew that I would have a stressful and confusing train ride ahead of me.

The train journey didn't disappoint. There is no form of hubbub and commotion like that of the Japanese railway network. Although some of the signs were available in English, there were many different lines, and I was surprised to discover that you had to book certain seats for certain lines and sit in the seat specifically assigned to you.

As I got into a carriage on the second train there was a commotion. I noticed that every person in that carriage was female, and they were all extremely angry. I had read about this in the guidebook, carriages designated just for women, and I had jumped slam bang into the middle of one of them and was in deep trouble.

"Sumimasen, Sumimasen," I apologised as best I could.

Eventually, a middle-aged lady in broken English comforted me. "You can stay. You can stay. We know you are foreign," and held my hand for a few moments. In the commotion I realised that I had missed my stop. I had been defending myself and doing my best to calm the carriage full of angry females and hadn't realised that I had gone past my stop at Kashiwa where I needed to change in order to get to Noda city.

I decided to get off at the next stop and then catch the train going back in the opposite direction. However, the women in the carriage had different ideas. They interpreted my trying to get off the train as backing out because they were upset, and did everything they could to keep me in the carriage.

"No, you can stay. You can stay."

It would be four stops before I was able to get off and catch the train back to Kashiwa, and from there I had to find the Noda Line.

By now, it was well past lunchtime, and I was finding it a very alien and confusing place to be. As I looked out of the window, none of the plant life or the building structures seemed remotely like anything that I was used to. I was feeling lost, confused and alien, and very homesick already.

There is a specific feel about Japan which is indescribable to someone who hasn't been there. This, to me, wasn't always a pleasant sensation – the very ancient alongside the extremely modern.

I got off at the stop for Noda. It was bitterly cold. On the station there was a vending machine dispensing a range of hot and cold drinks, many of which I had never seen before. The Japanese seem to be really into energy drinks of different types, and I had never before seen a machine that would serve freezing-cold Coca-Cola alongside hot corn soup. I was on a different planet. Japan was as far away from Norfolk, England, as I could possibly get...

Japan terrified me; it was so different and strange. From the moment I touched down I felt lost and confused. Nowhere has a buzz like Tokyo and nowhere has such an alien feel to the place. I made my way to rural Noda, catching trains to catch trains, and trying to negotiate my way by memorising the pictograms. Would I find the truth here in the birthplace of the Ninja?

I formulated my plan. I would approach this situation completely differently from my trip to America. I would keep a low profile and try to fit in. I knew there would be other westerners in search of the Grand Master's teachings. I would keep quiet, be respectful and observe all the etiquette of the Japanese.

Little did I appreciate that I knew nothing of Japanese culture; nothing at all!

Lost in Japan

I arrived at Noda station. I had been watching the stops like a hawk. I had no intention of getting lost in rural Japan with no knowledge of Japanese. I had already discovered that, unlike in every other country I had ever visited, there was no way you could rely on the local populace understanding any English. Japan had yet to be westernised. Noda station was cold. I stood around wondering what to do next.

Then it hit me! I was in Noda – the home of the last Ninja Grand Master Masaaki Hatsumi – I was going to see him! I was going to train with the direct source of all the knowledge we have now.

First I had to find my hotel, something that was going to be a challenge.

I was lost in Noda city, capital of soy sauce. Nobody spoke any English and I had neglected to bring any form of Japanese writing with the name of the 'ryokan' I was going to stay at. A ryokan is a traditional Japanese wash house. I had thought it would be very exciting to experience the Japanese culture as it really was.

I wandered around Noda for a good couple of hours, completely fixated by the strangeness and overwhelmed by confusion. I hoped to match the Japanese pictograms for the wash house in my mind's eye, or to match the picture I had seen of it on the internet with a physical building. I was silly to think this would work.

When the Student is Ready the Teacher will Appear!
In Japan, there is a special rule regarding pedestrians and bicycles. The rule is 'every man for himself'! Dodging bicycles and trains seems to be the first level of Ninja training for every level of Japanese citizen, no matter what their age.

I was completely lost. I had asked everyone I possibly could – people at the train station, people on the street, taxi drivers and police officers – but my Japanese was obviously far too bad.

But then something amazing happened. A brown American-built car pulled up beside me. There was another westerner in Noda! He smiled at me.

"Need any help?"

I could tell by his accent that he was American.

"Yes! I'm lost. I'm here to train at the Hombu dojo."

"Where are you staying?"

"The Azusa ryokan."

"Get in the car. I'll take you there."

As I talked to my new saviour, the guy introduced himself as Michael Pearce. I explained to Michael about my project, about the book, what my plans were, and that I had learned Ninjutsu from Karl and Shaun in a practical environment.

I also explained that I had gone and trained with Stephen Hayes, father of American Ninjutsu. Now I had come to Noda to discover the truth, having visited Ninja classes and found them inconsistent and less than useful in England.

"Well, it seems that you're following in Stephen Hayes' footsteps. The Azusa ryokan was where he first stayed!"

It was amazing to think of the coincidence that when Stephen Hayes had first come here he had stayed in the very same place we were heading to.

The car wended its way through very small back streets, sometimes almost touching the walls. I was wondering whether or not I would make it in one piece to my ryokan. Then it suddenly dawned on me. This westerner who I was talking to – how did he know who Stephen Hayes was? And most of all, how did he know what ryokan he had originally stayed in? Shit! I had just given myself away.

I said, "Are you part of the Bujinkan?"

"Yeah, I came here to study under Sensei," he replied.

"Who is your Sensei?"

"Masaaki Hatsumi."

Wow! This man was a student of the Ninja Grand Master. I

immediately asked him whether he could help me train, show me around, take me to the humble dojo. At that point, something miraculous happened. Michael Pearce indicated to me that he was a Freemason, something that I hadn't expected.

I had joined Freemasonry seven years ago. Freemasonry, for me, was a form of virtue, a spiritual path designed to help us be better men. The Freemasons are all brothers, and the possibility of running into one who practised Bujinkan, in Noda, was spectacular. I didn't even know that Freemasonry had got as far as Japan. To me, this was almost divinely sent.

We arrived outside the ryokan. I asked Michael if he knew any black belts or senior instructors that might help to guide me. There was a long silence. I asked him how long he had been training.

He answered, "Approaching 20 years."

"Twenty years under the Ninja Grand Master! What belt are you?"

"Twelfth."

A Twelfth belt in the martial arts is an extremely rare and precious thing. I couldn't believe my luck and immediately asked him if he would teach and guide me through my time in Japan. He agreed to do so, but he did warn me that this was going to be a very hard time, and would require a change within me.

I walked into the ryokan. Michael called me back out. He explained that in Japan you have to take your shoes off, and that there are special forms of slippers to wear whenever you go into a building. I removed my shoes and put on the glowing green plastic slippers, and he shouted something in Japanese as we walked through the door. A bright red-haired girl appeared. The whole place smelt of cigarette smoke. I paid for my room and was led upstairs.

The place, by western standards, was fairly small. It reminded me of a very low-budget bed and breakfast – not at all what I had imagined from the luxurious pictures of other ryokan I had seen in guidebooks and on the internet. As I was taken to my room I explained that I was here to be tested, and that I was going to do anything that I possibly could, to show my dedication in training in Jujitsu. The room basically contained tatami mats (a form of straw mat placed on the floor), a cushion for sitting on, and a table, nothing else.

"Well," Michael explained, "I asked for you to have a traditional Japanese room with tatami mats to sleep on, because I know that you're here to experience Japanese culture. Now, you've said that you'd like to be tested, and that you're here to develop your Ninja skills to your highest ability. Here's your first test. You're going back to Tokyo to train with

Master Hatsumi this evening."

I was overwhelmed with excitement. I was going to train with Hatsumi this evening, but I had missed a whole night's sleep. Surely it would take me a good hour and a half to get back?

"What time is it?" I asked. It was approaching 5 o'clock.

"You'd better get changed and get on the train."

I didn't know what to say. I would have to go. After all, I had said that I was willing to do anything. This was a test, an obvious first test, so I changed and got ready to go back to Tokyo. Michael gave me directions in the form of a small map with notes on it. And with that, he left.

Meeting with the Ninja Grand Master

On one side of the paper Michael had given me were directions to the Noda train station. The other side directed me to a place called the Budokan, which was a famous martial arts centre in Tokyo. I was very fearful as the train pulled away. I looked at the map again and again. I was about to meet the Ninja Grand Master at his class in Tokyo.

As the train pulled into Tokyo, I thought about Michael Pearce. There was something different about him. There wasn't a cell in his body that was trying to prove his status or rank; there he was, a Twelfth Dan in this martial art, and he had said nothing all the time I had been explaining my aims to him. That was something very special, very rare. I followed the directions to the Budokan, transfixed by the shops with their strange cartoons and depictions of animals everywhere. I found this aspect of Japanese culture quite exciting. The Japanese seem to use animals to depict everything. I even saw buses in the shape of anthropomorphised beings and depictions of cats shooting dogs on the side of police cars. In the toilets, sometimes there would be a picture of dung shouting instructions as to how you should conduct your hygiene habits.

As I approached the Budokan, I was overcome by the sight of this huge building. Martial artists of every build and type were gathered outside. It was about to happen: I was about to meet the instructor I had come all this way to see. I walked into the Budokan and asked for directions. I had managed to arrive a half hour early and was directed to the right place.

I went into the changing rooms, where I noticed there was a different pair of slippers which people were changing into. It seems in Japan there are different slippers for going to the toilet or going to the changing rooms, as well as for other types of rooms. I was the only person in the changing room. I donned my black *gi* (martial art suit), my green belt and my pair of indoor Tabis and moved into the dojo. I then, in embarrassment, went back to the changing room, took off my changing room slippers, and put on the normal slippers before returning to the dojo. Then removing all slippers, we went on the mats. I hate slippers.

I waited for what seemed like hours. The clock hands seemed to have stopped moving. Two or three Japanese students gathered. A couple of westerners who I struck up a conversation with were residents of Japan, one of whom had moved specifically to train with the Grand Master. I explained how nervous I was. Both had what seemed to be an Australian accent and were extremely relaxed. As I sat there, stretching, a peculiar sensation came over me, like an alarm bell ringing in my head – a danger sense, a tingling up my spine. Everything seemed wrong. I turned around and there he stood, the Ninja Grand Master.

He wasn't dressed in the big golden flowing clothes of Stephen Hayes or Rumiko, or other grand masters I had met. He wasn't dressed like a martial arts master at all; in fact he had purple hair and a fluorescent yellow top. But his presence hit me: a presence of power, of danger. I froze, overcome with fear. I had travelled across the world wanting spiritual guidance and martial instruction, but all this time I thought that I was coming to visit Yoda when in fact I was about to be taught by Darth Vader! This man was a killer, no doubt about it. If put in a position of danger, he could absolutely kill you. It felt like the presence of thousands of years of Japanese martial history was being expressed through him.

"Shi-kin hara-mitsu dai-ko-myo." He clapped his hands twice, bowed, recovered the bow, and bowed again. The whole class repeated and I copied. There weren't many people present. I had seen more people in classes in England, and certainly more at Dayton Quest. And then the class began.

My First Lesson in Japan

Hatsumi Sensei has a very specific way of teaching. He philosophises at the front of class and it is translated for those who don't speak Japanese. Someone was videotaping the whole event. He said today the subject of the lesson was going to be something called Shansin.

Shansin, he explained, was the ideal state of mind for combat, the state of mind that all warriors would have to invoke in order to be completely aware. He asked anyone in the group if they knew the song 'Temptation'. I was rather surprised to hear him reference something so western. He explained that Shansin was the same feeling that the song gives you. It literally translates as 'three hearts'. The three hearts of Shansin could mean mind, body and spirit. It could mean knowing what the opponent is thinking, knowing what you're thinking, and knowing the result of the two. *(See fig.45)*

Fig.45

We started training and I found myself partnered with two elderly Japanese masters. The exercise was a form of quick strike: the opponent came towards Masaaki Hatsumi and he raised his hand in one flowing motion to strike his adversary in the face. It looked pretty easy to me, so as my Japanese training partner came towards me I did the same. He looked horrified.

Then the problem started. I had two great Japanese masters as my training partners and I was doing something extremely wrong. The technique to me looked like punching very quickly whenever the person came towards you. I was doing that, but they were frustrated. They were trying to express something different to me. Then the next technique would appear something else, a defence against an arm grab, and the same kind of punch. I would do it again. The Japanese instructors were getting increasingly frustrated, sometimes even holding their heads in their hands. I was trying my best. I could not work out what was wrong, and the language barrier was destroying me. What was it that I was making the mistake on? How could I be so wrong?

Masaaki Hatsumi taught a technique, which was a flowing technique whereby an opponent grabs you, hits with one hand, and you in turn release his fingers, peeling them off by grabbing them and pulling his arm like a piece of rope. He explained the concept of pulling a rope. He talked about the ability to tie up the opponent, explaining that Shansin was the ability to remain untied by your emotions while tying the opponent. But he also warned that the process of tying up the opponent could in turn tie you up. Shansin was very much about rhythm and flow.

He said it was "like outliving jazz". I wondered if he meant outliving jazz as in living beyond the time of jazz, or whether this was a reference to the broken rhythm that jazz musicians use. This was about living that broken rhythm with a flow.

All of a sudden, the lesson changed. Suddenly he was demonstrating a technique with rope, of tying with rope. The opponent came at Hatsumi, grabbed the rope, and Hatsumi, in turn, tied him up securely into a hogtie kind of position in seconds. Once again, the opponent attacked Hatsumi, this time ignoring the rope. Again, the rope wrapped around the wrist of the opponent and he was tied up and on the ground in seconds.

"Now you play," said Hatsumi.

I hadn't the faintest idea where to start. I had practised Kusurifundo, the chain weapon, and had used that technique of wrapping the wrist, but didn't really know where to go from there. Once again, my Japanese training partners were frustrated. I could see that I was trying to use force to make up for my inadequacies, sometimes hurting them.

I was being a terrible student on my very first day. I kept asking as I knew that one of the instructors spoke some English. I kept approaching him, asking questions, but I could see he was starting to think that I was disrespectful. Eventually he said to me, with anger, "Too many questions; this is Grand Master's lesson!" I should have remembered that in Japan you don't question your instructors. I had failed miserably, but the worst was yet to come.

I had missed the next technique while approaching other people for help. I rejoined my Japanese training partners, hoping to see what the technique was to begin with. Suddenly, I lost my vision. Something had hit me in my left eye from nowhere and my eyes streamed with tears. It became obvious to everybody what had happened. Then came a segment of demonstration.

The technique was that of flicking something off the floor into the eyes of the opponent. My elderly Japanese training partner had picked up a Shuriken made of leather and flung it across the room into my eyes, expecting me, having observed the demonstration, to be ready to cover up. Not only had I failed miserably, I had made a laughing stock of myself.

The demonstration of techniques was most impressive. Under the pressure of the Grand Master's gaze, people would come up and display their techniques. This really did put them to the test. The pressure of demonstration would simulate the pressure of combat, being put on the spot. I could see that these martial artists were beyond anything I had ever seen before. Could I ever be that good? Could I ever fit in this class?

I could not understand anything. It was all too complicated, all too confusing. Everything the Grand Master said to me threw me. I didn't understand what he meant. He talked about the 'full nelson', and how it was a childish idea that it was used to lock the arms in position. How could this be? There was a subtlety in his movements that I couldn't pick up. The class ended and I felt devastated. I left without speaking to anyone, knowing that I would have to head back to Noda.

On the train, I met with two of the Australians that had arrived later on in the class. Then a third, female, Australian appeared bringing coffee and drinks. The head of the group projected a very positive force that could be felt reflected in his students. They were so friendly and full of smiles, but they did not realise what I was feeling inside. It was nice to meet a westerner. They talked to me. I asked them questions, but they were evasive, extremely evasive. I asked them which stop to get off at Noda and they gave me directions. They also gave me a cup of tea to take with me. I can genuinely say that they were three of the friendliest people I have ever met in the world.

As I got off the train, I realised two things. Firstly, that they had left with almost every piece of personal information about me that they could have possessed. Without my realising it, they had questioned me and found out exactly who I was, what my views were, why I was here, what I did for a living, who my family were, what kind of person I was, and the lifestyle I lived. I had left with just their names. I had been Ninja'd again!

Secondly, I realised that I had been given the wrong stop to get off at. This wasn't the stop that I recognised. I knew there were two train stations; I was on the opposite side of town and it was very late. Had they deliberately made me get off at the wrong stop? Was this some sort of Ninja way of teaching me not to trust people? Why had they done this to me? Was it deliberate? Was it a mistake? It seemed to me that whenever I encountered genuine Ninja I found myself questioning where their actions finished and fate began.

I started walking through the darkness. There wasn't a single person to be seen. I felt very confused. The world seemed to be moving very fast. It was freezing cold. I looked at my cup of tea. Was it the caffeine? Had my drink been drugged? Was it the lack of a night's sleep? What was going on here?

What looked like a pickup truck drove around the corner. A wailing song came from it as it passed me, with an open bonfire on the back of the van. I had never seen anything like it. There was a loudspeaker announcing something in Japanese.

He was the only person alive in Noda this late at night. I asked him directions. He had no idea what I was saying, my Japanese was so terrible. I was lost without any form of help, in the middle of Japan at night. What was I doing here? As I walked around Noda, I saw a stray dog eating from a bin. It was a beautiful golden brown colour; it looked almost like a fox. As I walked past an old lady came out to shoo it away from her bins.

She prodded it with a stick and scared it off. I felt sorry for the dog but carried on walking. There was no way that woman would be able to help me. I searched in and out of back alleys for over 4 hours, until at 1.30 in the morning a taxi driver saw my plight and stopped his car. He took his keys out and rattled them at me.

I didn't quite know what he meant. I explained to him that I was lost, but I couldn't make him understand. He rattled his keys again. Ahh! The key to my ryokan. I took out my key fob and it had the Japanese pictograms on them; he in turn read them and gave me a lift back to my bed. He didn't even charge me a penny. The Japanese, I later discovered, were all like this: the most helpful and polite race in the entire world. A Japanese person, on honour, will do their best to make sure you succeed and to help you to the best of their ability.

I got to the ryokan and sneaked inside. There were various notices which warned against making too much noise at night. I suspected that they had experienced drunk westerners also coming to train in martial arts there before, probably following in the footsteps of Stephen Hayes. I got up to my room, which was freezing cold. All I had to heat me was some form of fan heater attached to the roof. It had only one setting, so if I turned it on, it would take a huge amount of time to heat the air up and hot bugs that had been burnt in the fan heater would fall on my head.

Throughout the night I would wake up roasting hot and then go back to sleep, but I couldn't sleep for more than 5 or 10 minutes at a time. My mind was racing. My body was racing. I still wondered if the caffeine had affected me, if I had been drugged or if I was ill. Was it just my body clock confused by the flight, or adrenalin from the stress of the trip? Suddenly there was a rustling outside my window and as I peered out I saw a small shape. It was the stray dog! I opened the window and it approached me. I had made a friend!

It seemed almost magical. However, as I reached out to stroke it, the dog bit me and then ran away. I clutched my hand, covered in bite marks. Thankfully it hadn't pierced the skin too much. Oh God! Was I going to die of rabies as well? I didn't sleep a wink for the rest of the night. I can honestly say I have never felt so despondent. I had, in my heart, given up and I wanted to be home.

In the morning there was a big hubbub in the ryokan. I could hear a strange noise, like somebody hiccuping or trying to throw up. I felt very uncomfortable venturing outside the room to go to the toilet which was downstairs, but I really needed a shower.

Along the corridor I could see a line of Japanese businessmen cleaning their teeth. When they spat, they made the vomiting-style noise but in a very orderly fashion. As I went downstairs, I managed to find where I could clean my teeth, in private. But then I realised the terrible truth that the bath was communal! Men were smoking in the bath. It was a big hot tub. Around the bath were showers, where everyone was washing. I had to do it. I had to wash in front of everybody, and the response was not positive.

Little did I know at the time that having a tattoo represents membership of *Yakuza*, an infamous group of Japanese gangsters. The tattoo on my chest, a lotus flower, is a symbol of my heart remaining pure through all things, of maintaining standards of morality and virtue, no matter what. To them, it was a branding of me as a nasty, murdering gangster and nobody would speak to me. Everyone got out of the bath and left the room as fast as they could. I finished up and went to breakfast.

The people at breakfast were friendly and the Japanese television was insane! The food I ate was almost unrecognisable except for the raw egg. Raw egg was not a thing I was used to having served for breakfast, and definitely not on rice with raw fish. I couldn't identify what type of fish it was, but it was slimy and covered in a sauce that was tomatoey and salty and I did not like it. It came with a form of fermented soy beans which were covered in a mucous, sticky liquid, which to me was worse than Marmite. I ate as much as I could and then went back to my room.

Michael Pearce had given me a class timetable and had also promised to collect me in the morning, so I stood outside in the freezing cold waiting for him to appear.

Attitude Adjustment

As Michael and I drove along in the car, I said nothing. He, too, was silent for quite a while.

"In need of attitude adjustment?" he asked. He must have known how it had gone at the Hatsumi class, or maybe he had seen this happen to so many other people; it was par for the course.

"Yeah, how did you know?" I said.

"I could just see it coming. You need to go see Noguchi Sensei. And then we need to go to the Bonsai."

"Bonsai?" I thought to myself. What could Bonsai have to do with Ninjutsu in any shape or form? Maybe that's just what Michael did for a living? Perhaps he grew Bonsai? He didn't look much like a gardener, but looks can be deceptive.

We drove through Noda. Everything about Japan was so foreign and alien. When would I feel normal? It was not like visiting another country; it was like visiting another planet. I felt very confused, very lost and very distant. Driving through the back streets of Noda was like negotiating a maze. In Japan, they seem to have traffic wardens who are hired just to stand with a glowing stick and wave you on. They don't appear to do anything else. There were also lots of arcades and restaurants, all buzzing and full of activity. Intriguingly they had plastic models of food in the windows so you could see what was available to buy. Eventually, we arrived at Noguchi Sensei's house and dojo.

As we went into the small, quaint dojo, much like a western garage, I saw, standing before me, a man with a piece of bamboo in his mouth. Noguchi Sensei has a lightness, a humour to him; a feeling of joy and happiness. And the moment I entered the very room, I could feel it coming from him. My spirits were lifted just from being near him.

He was practising blowing darts. On his wall was a model of a person that he had drawn on a piece of cardboard at which he was firing darts, each one landing either on the heart or straight between the eyes.

"Do you want a go?" Michael asked me.

I took the blow darts from him, positioned it as I had seen Noguchi Sensei do, and fired my dart at the target. The dart didn't hit the target, but stuck in the wall in the background, very narrowly missing a picture of Hatsumi Sensei. Everybody laughed.

"Noguchi, I'm going to be teaching Martin the basics."

Perhaps if I hadn't gone to the Hatsumi class I would have questioned the validity of my needing to learn the basics. After all, I had already had three years of training in this art. But, having experienced the difference between my skill level and those in Japan, the basics seemed like a very good place to start.

We began by practising Kamae, the same stance movements I had learned in the US and Britain. Noguchi Sensei was a calm and gentle instructor. The stances used in Japan are far lower than those in To-Shin Do; however, the footwork was less exaggerated than in Britain, more like a poised cat ready to leap. Most of the combat appears from the normal standing position, but these Kamae, or attitudes, are used as a change from one place to another or as a springing action. In fact it was only at that moment I realised that the training in Japan was not like the classes in England in any way. I had been so in the moment I had never questioned that I was just learning.

Noguchi, a man in his 60s, was able to keep his stance so low that his bottom nearly touched the floor. I tried to match him but was unable to. After half an hour of this form of practice, my legs were like jelly. Noguchi said his goodbyes and left me with Michael, who said he was going to teach me to block and strike.

We practised blocking for what seemed like hours. My legs were barely taking my weight any more but then we came to striking.

How to Knock Someone Out With a Single Blow
(See fig.58)

Michael explained that in the Orient there was a far higher level of martial arts ability; knockouts were not achieved by the bouncing of the brain as in western boxing but through the disruption of blood flow to the brain through strikes to the neck.

I knew the Shuto strike. I looked at Michael and was pretty sure I could hit far harder than he could. Almost as if sensing my thoughts, he asked me to strike him.

"Hit me on the neck as hard as you can with a Shuto."

I paused, feeling a great resistance inside.

"Hit me on the neck as hard as you can with a Shuto!" he repeated.

In a street fight, no one is going to be waiting. I once again found myself surprisingly resistant. What if I hurt him? What if I knock him out? What if I cause permanent damage? A strike to the neck can move some vertebrae.

"Hit me! Hit me as hard as you can!"

Fig.58

I grabbed his arm to use as leverage. I knew this would give me a far harder strike than he expected. And, pulling with one hand, I hit him with every single cell of my body, with all my might, on the neck. I could see it rocked him and it hurt, but nothing more.

Michael explained to me that the strike was very strong, but the force was all wrong. It was more of a push than a strike. I had to learn how to hit with a snap – a snap that actually penetrated into the fibres of the neck; then I wouldn't have to hit as hard as before. He gestured with his hand, and made a slight strike to my neck.

Suddenly, in front of me was a green cloud. I could hear a strange noise in the distance, like bellows, breathing, whooshing. What was it? Where was I? What was this green mist? My vision started to clear; the green cloud was the mats lying in front of me. My hearing started to sharpen; the whooshing noise was me panting, me breathing deeply. I felt sad, disoriented, confused.

Michael Pearce had knocked me out. With that little strike to my neck, he had knocked me absolutely unconscious. I sat up, not knowing what to do except maybe cry. An apologetic Michael had made tea. As he sat me down he explained how I could learn to master the strike.

"When most think of the Shuto strike they think of someone breaking boards in a demonstration. Even from my own observations it seems this is the main place this strike is used. The reason for this is that most people don't actually use it enough to make it a viable tool in their martial practice. The other area where someone might see it or even use it is Kata (set forms of movement to simulate combat for the sake of individual practice). Still, the main drawback is not practising the strike in a way to make it of use.

"Here in Japan in the Hombu dojo the Grand Master and top instructors use it extensively. I would even venture to say it's *the* primary strike we do. I've found that the Shuto strike here is a very devastating strike. I know this because I've been and still do get hit with it often. Hatsumi Sensei has hit me so hard that my eyes have rolled up into the back of my head and I've been lying on the floor gasping for breath.

"So what I've found is that, as I said before, we don't use it enough to make it a truly devastating strike that can be relied upon as my Japanese teachers can. It's different than a punch in that there are far more elements involved. I'm only now beginning to understand this strike and because of that it's becoming a very dynamic destructive strike.

"When I say we don't use it enough what I mean is that although we do use it, we don't use it effectively or study how to use it. People, especially in the Bujinkan, have taken it for granted that the Shuto works without actually testing it. I'd also say that might be the case for many other arts. Hitting and breaking boards is a very different skill set than hitting someone. What I have noticed, though, is that the old masters sure knew how to hit and still do. As I mentioned, the Japanese masters here can drop you in a heartbeat with very little power.

"Lately at seminars I've told people to go hit each other just as hard as they can in the neck with a Shuto and see what happens. I'd say that out of all the seminars I've told students to do that, there've been probably five people that have actually fallen down from getting hit. Most just get pushed away.

"Now there are two main factors at work here, though. One is the psychological. What happens here from my own studies is this. As an example, let's say you're 30 years old and I tell you to hit someone as hard as you can. Now this someone is a training partner and probably a friend. First thing you will think to yourself, 'I don't want to hurt my buddy.' By the very nature of this thought you'll not be able to, no matter how hard you try; nor will it be an effective strike. The second factor I have found in my studies is this. All your childhood you're told by your parents not to hit. Society tells us that it's wrong to fight or hit people. So now I come in and tell you to hit someone. After 30 years of this kind of conditioning what chance do you have of breaking that within 5 minutes? None.

"So with those factors in mind I began to study my teachers and myself. What I found is that they are different in these areas. In the first area they try to hit, not necessarily hard, but effective always. They train like it was a real situation, so they're getting rid of the 'it's my buddy' mentality every time they train. Also I know they're going to hit hard and so when they do I'm not offended or whatever. I enjoy the chance to feel it and train with them. Please remember, though, there's a difference between hitting hard and hitting with force and poor ability.

"By training every time as if it's real, they're little by little taking off that filter that's been forced in place over their entire lives. In this way their strikes become more and more effective as they get better in their movements and understanding of their art.

"Another point that's important to understand in striking with the Shuto is that it's a strike not a push. I've often observed that when someone tries to use the Shuto the only visible effect is the *Uke* (training partner) being pushed away or across the room. This is a push, not a strike. When Sensei or the Japanese *Shihan* (expert instructor) strike me I fall straight down. I can't think of any one time where I was pushed away.

I've found that the main reason that most tend to make it a push and not a strike is the distance and timing used when trying to strike. Most hit way too close and when they've already completed their movement. So the strike becomes a weak push at best.

"You have to study the whole body to understand how to make this strike truly devastating. You need to understand the best points of distance. You have to study the body dynamics of your arm, shoulder and body to know where the most effective alignments are so that you can use them in your strike. What are the optimum body alignments for the optimum strike? Once you understand these, you'll then be able to not only strike but also destroy an opponent with the Shuto. The strike needs to hit the artery on the neck on a parallel plain. This in turn sends the blood pressure rocketing and the brain's automatic response is to turn off, which makes you collapse as an emergency attempt at compensation."

This was the end of my second lesson in Japan.

Bonsai – Learning how to Approach Budō

On the way to the Bonsai farm one day, Michael gave me another talk.

"Budō isn't something you can rush; it's something you work at. You chisel away, every year of your life, every day of every year of your life. Budō is a lifelong ambition. It's not something you can just charge at and master."

I had never heard the term used before, and Michael must have picked up on my lack of comprehension.

"Budō is a Japanese term, a compound of the root *bu*, meaning 'war' or 'martial', and *dō*, meaning 'path' or 'way'. Specifically, *dō* is derived from the Buddhist Sanskrit *mārga*, meaning 'the path to enlightenment'. The term refers to a process of philosophical critique and investigation. *Dō* signifies a 'way of life'; in the Japanese context it's a discipline cultivated through a given art form. So rather than being a martial art it's a way of life, a path of self-development. In modern times Budō has no external enemy, only the internal enemy – one's ego – that must be fought."

He looked at me.

"The approach you're using is all wrong. You're burning yourself out in these tiny bursts of effort. It's time to show you a little bit about the Japanese culture. I used to work on a Bonsai farm here and I'll show you some examples of my work and we can learn a little bit about Bonsai."

I must admit, at that time I didn't want to learn about Bonsai. I was more focused on the knockout blow, imagining what it would be like to get to hit this off switch on the opponent so easily, to end the fight with such speed.

I did, however, agree that it was a good idea to learn a little bit about the Japanese culture, and to spend some time with Michael to get to know him. He had a different air from Stephen Hayes, an air that was reflected from his teacher, Hatsumi Sensei, of viciousness and of danger. He was a warrior through and through. During the many times I trained with him I could see an intensity bubbling inside him but that he was holding back. However, when he started to handle the Bonsai, I saw a different type of person.

Michael continued, "Bonsai is an art that goes back thousands of years and it's not specific to Japan. We know that in the ancient Egyptian culture they also used to grow very small trees, ensuring that they didn't get to their full size by using a very similar process to that used by the Japanese now.

"The word 'Bonsai' is a Japanese pronunciation of a Chinese term 'Penzai', which means a tray-contained pot plant. But, of course, now we just use it to mean undersized trees."

(See fig.47)

Michael showed me some of his masterpieces, which truly were beautiful and far more outlandish than the trees I had seen before in pictures; they were amazing works of art in their own right.

He explained that the process of making Bonsai was to take a cutting,

Fig.47

or indeed grow a seed, from the right type of tree. Then you provide a certain material for it to grow in, depending on what type of look you wanted to get.

The next technique would involve a process called layering. Layering is a technique in which rooting of the tree or cutting, usually a branch from a bigger tree, is encouraged to grow into an independent entity, then you start to prune it into shape. This can take a lot of trimming and has to be done for many years. The small size of the tree is achieved by wiring its roots, limiting its nutrition and also by pruning and careful shaping.

He showed me a tree he had been working on, indicating the wires holding the tree branches into place. I asked him when the tree would be ready. He explained to me that the tree was in fact five years old.

"You see, Bonsai is an ongoing process; the work is alive and therefore it never ends. So you always have an opportunity to change, improve and maintain the shape of the Bonsai. Not just a deadwood," he pointed out. "It was deliberately created for a certain effect."

At that moment something suddenly hit me. I had been so blind. When Michael talked about attitude adjustment, I hadn't realised – or hadn't connected – the fact that 'attitude' is the word the Ninja use for their fighting positions, Kamae, and that we had spent the whole of the day adjusting these positions.

Earlier, Michael had told me that it would take many years for me to get myself into the stance of Noguchi Sensei and that I should be patient. He had explained that this was an ongoing work, a lifelong work. He had then taken me to the Bonsai farm, where the Bonsai also were ongoing works. Their attitude, or their position, was being adjusted year upon year – mostly by removing rather than adding things. I had come to Japan to collect new techniques to discover the truth. Michael wanted me to remove my bad habits and to focus on adjusting my attitude, both in my mind and in my body; they were intrinsically connected.

I tend to stand up tall, have very vertical stances, be very upright. I don't bend my knees much. My legs tend to pull in on themselves. These are all symbolic. My pride kept my stance upright. My self-focus pulled me into myself.

Michael had taken me to the Bonsai farm to teach me, by analogy and by example. I don't know if he expected it to sink in consciously or subconsciously, but the lesson was the same. Instead of racing towards one goal and expecting it to be the end, this was an ongoing daily practice for the rest of my life.

Ninja, too, wasn't something to do or to learn; it was something I had to be. Ninja – the art of enduring. We are all enduring; we are all learning to live and trying to live the best we can. So Ninjutsu is what we are all practising; it's just that a Ninja does it consciously and with far greater efficiency.

As my time continued in Japan I found this was the approach that all the masters used. There was no meditation or *Kuji-in* practice, although I saw pictures of these practices on the walls. The whole attitude was summarised in the phrase used before each class.

Shi-kin Hara-mitsu Dai-ko-myo

"Shi-kin hara-mitsu dai-ko-myo.

As the first class started, I noticed a routine that seemed to be very special. The candles were always lit at the beginning and everybody lined up and knelt, and then they all clapped twice, bowed, clapped once, and bowed again.

"Shi-kin hara-mitsu dai-ko-myo," they all repeated in unison.

That evening, I asked Michael Pearce what it meant.

"Every action presents a potential key to enlightenment," was his answer.

Every action. That was very interesting. This was the motto of the Ninja school, and indeed this was the attitude I found summarised in Japan.

Enlightenment, to them, was in Budō, was in the physical martial arts, and although they could see some positive aspects about meditation and other spiritual practices, they didn't really focus on them, and it wasn't taught. I thought this was a pity, but I could understand their way of doing things.

It was all about learning from the action, learning from the physical art. I felt that this was a very useful approach and something I should incorporate into my training. However, the tools I had learned in Dayton, of meditation, of *Kuji-in*, I believed were so invaluable, it really would benefit anybody. They were tools that I was going to need to continue to use if I was going to survive my time here.

Never Show Your Weaknesses

When I was a teenager and overzealous with my martial arts training, I once caused a tear in the supporting muscles in my right shoulder. These are called the rotator cuff and are there to keep the shoulder joint in place. It was an extremely debilitating and painful injury which made it very hard to train physically or to do the things I loved. But through extreme hard work and arduous exercise routines given to me by a physiotherapist, I managed to right this wrong and heal the injury.

In Japan, however, fate was against me. During one lesson a training partner put me in a shoulder lock, which caused a slight dislocation of my shoulder for a few moments. Once again the muscle had torn. I was in agony.

I was aware of what happened and was very nervous that this injury would prevent me from taking part in the classes for the rest of the week. The next morning, I took time to talk to the instructor before the class and explained my shoulder problem.

The teacher responded, "Of course, of course, we will be gentle. We will not hurt the shoulder. Of course."

The class started. The focus of the class was shoulder locks. For 2 hours, the instructor tortured me, either directly or via training partners. Everything was designed to cause pain to that injury. It was terrible. I felt angered, upset and confused. Why would this man do this to me?

At the end of the class, there was silence. We had finished bowing, and everybody was about to leave. The instructor stood up.

"Never show your weaknesses to anyone. This is an important lesson."

After 2 hours of the most excruciating anxiety and pain, it was a lesson I would always remember!

The Ninja should appear to be normal. No one should know whether he is a strong man, a weak man, a martial artist, or anything about him. He should not give any information away. This was something that the Australian Ninja I had met at the beginning of my trip had certainly learned, and something I, too, would now never forget.

The Secret of Shanshin

Over the next few days, I appeared at every lesson at the Hombu dojo. I met the *Shihan* or senior black belts there and each had his own different character and manner. As fate would have it, there were barely any westerners in town. In fact at most classes which I attended, I was the only westerner there and it made communication extremely hard.

One lesson was with Master Nagato Sensei. Nagato was a big, friendly man and had the same beautiful feeling of happiness and pleasantness around him as Noguchi Sensei. I remember at the beginning of the class he stood forward and made the same secret signs with his hands that Stephen Hayes had. The feeling in the room again changed in exactly the same way.

Nagato turned to me and said, "Martin, you have to learn to be a big man without being big outside. You must view yourself as a vessel of this art, a container for its tradition. You must hold it inside yourself."

Without pause, he announced that this class would be about the

Sanshin no Kata. Shansin, as already discussed by Hatsumi Sensei, means 'three hearts'.

Shansin, Nagato explained, was a state of combat focus that a warrior must cultivate, and that this was an extremely important state of awareness for the whole of Budō, or the warrior art.

There is a specific set of exercises, *Sanshin no Kata*, which involves a block and a strike corresponding to each element. The movement was a flowing movement, backwards and forwards.

It suddenly dawned on me that in a previous class, that first class with Hatsumi, this was what the Japanese teachers had been trying to explain to me. I had been striking with a great force and they had pointed to the clock on the wall to show me the pendulum moving backwards and forwards. I had thought at the time they were indicating that the class was coming to an end and that we didn't have much time, when in fact they were wanting me to move like the pendulum.

The *Sanshin no Kata* is also known as the Gogyo (Five Great Elements). Each strike corresponds to one of the elements:

Chi (Earth) Sanshin Ken (Three Finger Strike)

Sui (Water) Jodan Uke (Upper Block) and Omote Shuto Kubi (Outer Shuto Strike)

Ka (Fire) Jodan Uke (Upper Block) and Ura Shuto Kubi (Inner Shuto Strike)

Fu (Wind) Gedan Uke (Lower Block) and Boshi Ken (Thumb Strike)

Ku (Void) Gedan Uke (Lower Block) and Meysubushi (Distraction) and Keri (Kick)

Chi no Kata (Earth)

The attacker punches to the face. The defender drops back from Shizen diagonally backwards into Ichimonji, blocking with his left arm while the right arm moves backwards in a flowing motion in line with the right leg. The defender then steps forward and his arm swings up in a pendulum-like manner while the blocking arm swings back down, and the little finger and thumb join to form a Sanshinken (three-finger strike) that strikes under the chin.

Sui no Kata (Water)

Again this Kata starts with a punch to the head. The defender drops back from Shizen diagonally backwards into Ichimonji and performs a Jodan Uke (upper block). Again the arms pass in a pendulum motion. The defender then steps forward and performs an Omote Shuto Kubi to the opponent's neck.

Ka no Kata (Fire)

The attacker punches to the head. The defender drops back from Shizen diagonally backwards into Ichimonji and performs a Jodan Uke (upper block) then steps forward and performs an Ura Shuto Kubi, hitting the opponent's neck on the other side.

Fu no Kata (Wind)

In this Kata the attacker kicks. The defender then drops back from Shizen diagonally backwards into Ichimonji and performs a Gedan Uke (lower block). He then steps in and performs a Boshi Ken (thumb strike) to the attacker's solar plexus or pit of the stomach.

Ku no Kata (Void)

Like the previous Kata this form starts with the attacker kicking. The defender drops back from Shizen diagonally backwards into Ichimonji and performs a Gedan Uke (lower block). His hand comes up in the same flowing motion as the other strikes but he simply opens his hand, palm facing forward, to distract his opponent. He then follows through with a front kick.

The whole of the Kata or routine was about flow; one arm goes up, the other goes down. The whole form is practised with total focus and calmness in order to get into the combat focus state of mind – a focus I started to take into my daily life. However, there was something more in this set of techniques. Something I saw that others didn't. A code!

It was the first technique that set alarm bells ringing. Was it not coincidental that in the first technique, named after the Earth element, the Earth finger joined with the thumb? Then it hit me that the same was true of the Wind strike, but in the Void element technique we joined no fingers. The Shuto position allowed you to easily touch either the Water or Fire finger. This was perfect for evoking the elemental force with your strike. I was convinced I had discovered some of the underlying system in the Ninjutsu. I told Michael Pearce of my discovery, but he was unconvinced and disinterested. He explained that the elements were just a simple counting system and that things were different here in Japan.

Ten Chi Jin

In Japan the classification of the martial art syllabus is not by the four elements. However, the four elements are mentioned within the teachings but very subtly. I was told to forget about them; they were not effective or useful; the syllabus used in Japan was of a different structure.

The classification system used – the Ten Chi Jin – is a strategic one and is designed to make you think about all areas of any situation. Ten Chi Jin means 'heaven', 'earth' and 'man'. This system comes from the Chinese Daoist system of writings and is something that I was aware of in my previous studies.

'Heaven' represents both the weather and environmental situations, but could also symbolise the philosophy and outlook of the people involved; 'earth' represents the physical distance and the practicalities involved in the matter; whereas 'man' represents the social interactions and pressures upon the person.

So, for example, if we were to apply these three principles to a self-defence situation, we would immediately want to make sure that we were using the principles of heaven to our advantage. We would position ourselves so that the sun was behind us in order that our opponent would be in the glare of the sun as he tried to engage us, or perhaps, if it was raining, we would position ourselves so that we were free of obscuring rainfall.

We could also position ourselves so that psychologically we had an advantage whether in or out of view. This brings us to the earth principle, whereby we would be paying attention to distance. If the opponent was a large, strong man we might want to stay at a distance, or indeed get so close that his strength couldn't affect us. We might want to ensure that physically we were standing higher or that he was on an uneven surface.

And finally, man. We may want to take into account his psychological processes or where he would feel uncomfortable in combat. Maybe we would lead him into a circumstance where his other enemies would be, or where peer pressure would lead him to do the wrong thing.

Strategically, this could be applied and used to understand any situation.

So, for example, if someone you know is having relationship problems, you can consider which of these factors are affecting him. Could it be that the heaven element is causing problems, that perhaps the environment they find themselves in is not conducive to their nature? Perhaps his girlfriend is foreign and doesn't like the climate. Maybe he finds it uncomfortable being cramped inside a house, or he takes her to the wrong environment when they spend time together and should take her to more pleasant surroundings. Perhaps mentally his attitude and their ideals of a relationship are incorrect and need to be changed.

If there are financial problems it may be earth principles in action. Perhaps the distance physically between them is too much, or too little. Maybe by altering these physical circumstances the mental attitude will change easily.

And finally, socially. Could there be problems to do with how she is interacting with his friends or family, or how he interacts with hers? Perhaps there are problems with how he presents her to his family and how social opinion reacts to what they are doing.

By considering heaven, earth and man, I found this opened up another layer of creativity, something additional to the elements. When considering the two in tandem you can work out solutions and possibilities to make virtually anything happen, to make virtually anyone do what you want.

The more I continued on the Ninja path, the more I began to appreciate that Ninjutsu is the study of and love of strategies: the strategies of making people do what you want. This really is the way.

How Ninjas Teach

So my routine in Japan started to form. I was really lucky, as the classes had very few people attending them, and those who were there were extremely skilled in the arts I was trying to learn. My day would start at 6 o'clock in the morning, and I would get out of bed early so I could use the bathroom before the other guests in the ryokan had woken up.

In Japanese ryokan, it is normal to have a communal bath in the morning. The routine is that everyone gets under a shower and scrubs themselves to the highest degree of physical purity attainable by man. And then, in turn, everyone settles into an extremely hot, bubbling tub, which has pictures on the wall of pleasant mountainous scenes, the kind of thing that wouldn't be found in Noda.

After my morning bath, which most of the time I took alone, I would make my way to the breakfast hall, wondering what I would be eating today. Breakfast might consist of anything from western meatballs, spaghetti or cold cuts of unidentifiable meat, to raw egg on rice, squid guts in tomato sauce, eels or fish – even little baby fish, which I wondered whether they had been born yet in order to be that size. The menu was spectacularly different from anything I had ever had before. And though a challenge, it was all part of the experience. I was having a genuine Japanese adventure.

Then I would tank up on as much tea as possible before getting on my bike and cycling through the freezing cold, busy streets of Noda to the Hombu dojo, awaiting my first lesson of the day.

Martial arts training in Japan is unlike any training I have ever seen in the west. It consists of a demonstration of a martial technique in a simulated combat circumstance. You are then given a partner, who will attack you in the prearranged way, normally with gusto, and you, in turn, should defend using the technique that has been demonstrated. It is far rougher than in other countries in which I have experienced training, and you really need to learn how to hold your teeth so they don't clank together when you get hit, something which Noguchi Sensei was kind enough to teach me at the beginning.

The idea is that there is intent in the attack and in the defence. If you don't finish the technique, then you should do something to eliminate your opponent. You should never freeze. If you freeze in practice, you will freeze in combat. There were no long Kata, no fancy forms, no beautiful footwork. The whole point was to defend and attack from the normal position, only using the Kamae as a means to gain leverage or deliver a forceful attack – something that had been totally misinterpreted in England.

The arts in Japan are very beautiful. Not externally, but internally. Whenever Masaaki Hatsumi taught he would display his ability at free-form Japanese painting. He explained that we should develop arts and Budō – meaning martial arts – in equal balance, to keep ourselves balanced people. This is something which I have come to realise is completely true. Hatsumi had developed his painting; Stephen Hayes, his poetry; and Michael Pearce's great love was falconry.

There were normally four classes in a day, each taking 2 hours, which is twice as long as the lessons in Dayton or in Britain. They were not as intense, and there was a break for tea halfway through, during which we could talk to the instructor. I felt that all the Japanese instructors were very deep, spiritual, dedicated people, and it was a real honour to spend time with them.

My greatest guide was, of course, Michael Pearce who I learned had bought a one-way ticket and left America for Japan as a teenager in order to follow his dream of learning from the Ninja Grand Master. He was a restless fiery character and had dedicated his life to the study of many different arts: Ninjutsu, traditional Japanese dance, Bonsai, and even Native American shamanism. In many ways he seemed to me more shamanic than anything else – haunted in some ways and empowered by the same passions that pained him. His focus on his areas of interest eclipsed anything else in life and it was due to this that he made a great teacher, completely focused and dedicated.

However, I was starting to have problems with my training. The movements that were being used in Japan were far finer than those I was used to. I had been used to making dramatic, broad, sweeping and powerful movements, both in striking and dodging. The Japanese masters were moving just centimetres, something I was finding frustrating to try to imitate. I didn't seem to have the small muscle movements, or micro-motor control that they had. I had habits from other martial arts which were getting in the way.

I would normally find 10 minutes between classes to run and grab some lunch – which would normally be a packed lunch – nearby. By the end of the day, I was always completely physically exhausted. I would return to my ryokan and do my meditation before heading off to see Michael Pearce, who would debrief me on what I had done that day and give me advice. Michael, who appeared to be nocturnal, would always be there to help me and to translate matters which I found confusing during the day. I sometimes took a photo of my breakfast for his entertainment, and it was nice to find out what I had actually eaten! It was wonderful to have his guidance.

The evening would be spent talking of Ninjutsu, training, martial arts and the spiritual world. It also included drinking beer and eating squid legs. Squid legs, or squid tentacles, as I suspect they should be called, are served as a snack in Japanese taverns, rather like we would have crisps served in Britain.

There would be an ongoing war between Michael and myself: while I attempted to get home to the ryokan to sleep ready for the new day, he would like to stay up all evening, talking and training. Some nights he would buy a bottle of Scotch and we would get outrageously drunk. "Even moderation in moderation," as Michael used to say! I was getting more tired by the day.

Many nights, I was having just 2 hours' sleep. I had to get up for my lesson in the morning – Michael didn't. I was getting more and more run down. On the way back to my ryokan, I would always stop at the Shinto shrine in the city and make a prayer to the Kami to help me with my training.

This continued for almost two weeks. One day I was in a class and found myself tired beyond tiredness. I had never experienced a feeling like this. I was barely able to move my body. The bike ride that morning had almost killed me. I hadn't been eating as much as I normally do and the late nights, early mornings and the pure stress of being in a different place had got to me.

I remember one class when a technique was being displayed, and Michael Pearce was filming it. Noguchi Sensei was an amazing man, both in persona and in martial practice. On this particular day, he was showing a technique of evasion and he asked someone to step forward to kick him. *(See fig.59)*

He showed a back step, which moved him just inches away from the kick. He called me up to do the same, so I decided to surprise him. Instead of doing a normal Bujinkan Ninjutsu-style front kick, I would do something from a different martial art.

Rather than kicking him in the waist as was taught in this art, I would do something I had never seen anyone do in the Japanese dojo. I was going to kick through his head with a high kickboxing-style roundhouse kick at lightning speed to see what he would do.

He did the same movement, without any form of surprise or reaction. I was truly amazed. But this wasn't the last time that Noguchi Sensei was to amaze me in the whole class, and a revelation was about to come forward that would make me reflect on the whole of my visit to Japan.

We started practising the darting movements. My partner was a nerdy-looking Japanese boy wearing glasses who was just beginning. He had great energy, and was very directed; I, however, was barely in the room.

Again and again, we drilled the same darting movements. In Japan, it is not unusual to practise the same technique for over 2 hours and the Japanese are truly tireless. Only westerners get bored and seem to feel the need to vary the technique while they practise. The Japanese have a focus, a drive and a discipline that we can all look up to, and since my visit I have endeavoured to incorporate that into my martial art training. The focus on detail and the focus on perfecting the technique in hand are remarkable.

However, on this particular day I was finding that extremely hard and when he struck at me, I could barely move my legs. Instead of a dodge, or even a step, a small shuffle came out of my legs. Michael Pearce took note of it from the other side of the room. He watched as the same thing was repeated again and again – and then I heard something. Something just on the edge of my hearing, said between him and one of the Japanese instructors.

Fig.59

My Japanese training partner laughed. "He just said you can sleep now!"

All this time, he had been keeping me up deliberately. He knew that I had far too much energy, far too much fire, and instead of perfecting the movements, I was treating it as a form of physical exercise. My energy and my enthusiasm had been working against me. In order to show me the other way of moving, he had to work together with the instructors to tire me out. Day by day, I was being physically put through my paces. During the day, I would have lessons with Noguchi, Oguri and the other senior instructors and, of course, Masaaki Hatsumi, the Ninja Grand Master. Then in the evening, Michael would be full of energy, tiring me out with activities. Sometimes it would be falconry, sometimes paragliding; most of the time it was sitting, talking and displaying martial arts movements. The tiredness had become my ally, and I started to use it as such.

My technique started to improve and I found it easier to follow what was happening. I noticed that there were many levels of subtlety behind the techniques that westerners missed. Whenever there were more than two or three westerners in a class, the whole style of training would change. A technique which involved brushing the eye with one's fingers, striking the person and using that movement to become an arm hold would simply be an arm hold. I began to see why Michael disliked crowded classes.

You Have to Steal This Art

One of the things about training with such great masters is that you start to learn by observing the Ninjutsu in what they do. After all, in every action is the chance of enlightenment. Hatsumi Sensei teaches Ninjutsu in every action that takes place. By watching these actions, you could learn a lot more than by any other method. Hatsumi kept everybody off balance and confused.

They were always searching for what was coming next. To make things harder, Hatsumi's words are very deep, allegorical and have many layers of meaning. For example, I remember one occasion when he chastised students for coming to the lesson with a cold. He then went on to talk about the use of chemical weapons and how you can carry poisons on the wind. He talked about the power of gossip and fear, and of how it can spread like a disease. He talked about how you can defeat opponents without having to see them or be at risk yourself. After the class I was horrified to hear that some of the students thought he was implying that the illness was as a result of a chemical warfare attack by terrorists or the west! They failed to see the hidden meaning.

I noticed the western students were always fighting amongst each other and vying for status. Only the true focused students like Michael Pearce remain directed towards the true higher teachings. These tended to be the old guard who had been in Japan many years. Everyone else was running around, madly trying to prove things and attacking others. I started to think the myths of Ninja being evolved from Tengu were true!

I didn't like this at all, but in one way it did dawn on me that this is an extremely efficient method as it filters out people who are not truly there and dedicated. Whether this is a natural production of people's natures or is deliberately produced by Hatsumi is open to debate. One of the things I found with all Ninja masters is that when they truly work you don't know whether it is them working or something of the universe.

Often, during my stay in Japan, I would ask about different Ninja skills. I would ask about meditation and would be told that this was no longer practised as in the old days. I asked about stealth, about acrobatics, about the other traditional Ninja skills. Once again, I was told that these were no longer taught in Japan. I enquired as to why, and different people gave different answers. As time went on, I became convinced; the reason was to do with what westerners had originally done with many of these stealth skills.

Karl and Shaun were perhaps a good demonstration of why they had stopped teaching these arts! It had led people to misuse them. People had got drunk in Noda and caused problems. People had gone away and used stealth incorrectly.

Now the Japanese felt that it was not a positive thing to teach an art that included poisoning with herbs, pick pocketing and silent walking to westerners. I remember one moment in a class with Masaaki Hatsumi. He was talking about wrapping the opponent up like rope, the theme of tying opponents. Then he said something very poignant.

"You need to steal their intention away from them. You need to steal the combat." He paused for a few moments. "Ninjutsu is not anything you can be taught, or can be learned. You have to steal Ninjutsu."

It dawned on me at that moment that he was correct, that nowadays many of these arts weren't being taught, but you could still steal them, and there were many ways in which this could be achieved. You could, of course, learn the art of silence by logical extrapolation from the physical type of Jutsu you are being taught. You could go to students who had previously learned these arts. Maybe you could find a way to convince a modern Japanese master to disclose them to you. Perhaps you could trick him into revealing them by asking him questions about historical texts on stealth.

Either way, Ninjutsu is something that you have to steal. You have to go wherever the skill takes you. Sometimes the answers a Ninja master would give were deliberately designed to discourage the student from learning something before he was ready.

For example, Michael Pearce told me that when he first came to Japan he asked about the *Kuji-in*. Masaaki Hatsumi responded by saying, "That was just movie stuff." And yet at the same time, there was a picture of him with his master, Takamatsu, performing the *Kuji-in* on the wall behind him!

He told Michael it was movie stuff because it was, for him, at that level of development. Perhaps this was the reason why whenever I asked about stealth, the answer was that this was old-fashioned training; modern technology and techniques had got far beyond what the original Ninja were doing, and that you could learn that elsewhere.

Once again, the Ninja were giving the answer which would discourage the student from asking further questions or from seeking extra tuition. I think many westerners have betrayed the responsibility that comes with these skills and because of that, the Japanese are now extremely reluctant to share skills that could be misused by westerners.

But how to steal it? I remember complaining to one of the long-term students that they did not teach stealth in class and that they didn't seem to use the weapons much. In Japanese culture you don't ask, so it's a difficult position. I mentioned to him about Hatsumi's 'stealing the art' comment and he simply responded, "You are never going to be able to do that. How the hell would you be able to do that?" To him it was not possible. But I had really paid attention to my elemental training and my Ten Chi Jin. My strategic powers were developing daily, so I focused my mind and drew together my aims. I would learn both stealth and the art of dodging throwing stars. *I would steal these arts from the masters.* This would be an exercise to see if it was possible.

How to Dodge Throwing Stars

During my time in Japan I was always at the dojo. I used to turn up hours early for the class and just practise. It was during this time that I hatched my master plan. The whole feel of the training in Japan was playful; Hatsumi often used the phrase, "OK, now play!" in his lessons. It was this playfulness I would aim to take advantage of.

I knew that two young Japanese students were turning up to this particular class as they did every week and they would be part of my master plan. When they appeared, they were already in good spirits and surprisingly boisterous for Japanese. I noted the time on the clock was getting close to the time the instructor would arrive. So I grabbed a pile of leather practice throwing stars and, with a playful expression, started to pelt the two unsuspecting students. They instantly returned fire and a war started. Soon other piles of practice throwing stars were gathered and all hell broke out. Then the instructor arrived on the scene. I could see him opening the door.

It was the moment of truth as to how he would respond when he came in to three students rolling, jumping and throwing stars around the place. Would he be angry or amused? He walked into the room and a throwing star whizzed past his head. There was initial surprise and then... he smiled.

We continued to fight and the instructor tried to formulise and control what we were doing. First he got one of us to hold a staff and we threw stars at him while he stood with his body sideways on and moved at angles to make sure the staff always shielded him. This was to demonstrate how you only had one small surface area to cover if you turned your body to the side.

Then came the real training. Standing in *Hira no Kamae* and using what To-Shin Do practitioners would call 'air footwork', we took turns pivoting our body backwards to avoid the stars, which was surprisingly effective. We were taught that if you had to, you could use your open palm with your fingers pulled back to literally slap the stars out of the air before they hit you. This we found we hardly needed to do as the backwards pivot dodge was so remarkably effective. I had succeeded in learning the legendary Ninja Shuriken dodging skill!

The next challenge was harder – stealth. I knew that many people had tried to learn stealth in the last few years, but they had always failed and got the same answer: that these skills are really outmoded. "We don't teach those arts anymore. Things have moved on since then. The modern military really have got better ways of doing things now. You can go to them to learn."

I wanted to compare my training with Karl and Shaun with what was known here. I had to work out a way of making them show me, so I formulated a plan. I had to use all my elements and my 'heaven', 'earth' and 'man'. I needed to find the perfect motivator, the perfect environment and social situation. I needed to get in the mind of the instructor.

I thought about the teachers. I would choose one who loved history. I would choose one who loved the intellectual study of the art. I would bring my translation of the ancient Ninja text the *Bansenshukai*. I would also bring a book written by a very unreliable source who interpreted the methods of stealth and a few of the other techniques. I would bring a gift of English tea to give to the master halfway through the lesson; this would make the break longer than planned to give me the chance to have the conversation, and it would also trap the bilingual students in the conversation in case I needed them. I would then discuss the ancient names for techniques and move the subject to stealth and show what was taught by the rival authority.

This I hoped would have the correct effect of making the teacher feel genuinely happy, being able to talk over a subject he loved with a student, amongst a sea of those less interested. He would be grateful for the tea, which would add to his happiness, and all this would lower his guard. I would act as if my interest was in the historical interpretation of the methods of walking and argue the comparison of the ancient terms to modern methods. Hopefully this would bring about the information I hoped for, and I might even be able to get a demonstration.

The class formed and I took a deep breath. Could I subtly steer the entire class into the direction I wanted and gain education in subjects I was told were no longer taught?

I practised hard and tried to keep my focus on the job in hand. This needed to seem natural. When the break came the plan sprang into action and unfolded exactly as I had hoped. The teacher was overjoyed at his tea from the royal household and even more overjoyed to see the *Bansenshukai*! With a sense of childlike wonder we went through every step, every detail and every phrase of terminology. I demonstrated what I thought the walking methods in the text were, and he, in turn, either corrected my technique or, if I had got the wrong step, demonstrated the technique I was missing. This continued until the end of the lesson. By the end I had managed to learn all the traditional lessons in stealth from one of the longest-standing students of the last Ninja on earth. I had been successful. I had also shown how powerful my strategic training had been.

However, there was more to this lesson. The more I thought about it, the more I realised stealing didn't just have to be done literally; it was about the attitude needed to grasp the art. To steal something you have to go in with a very clear aim of exactly what you are after. Go in, grab it, run off with it and make it your own. You need to go into the situation knowing exactly what you want, how you are going to get it and where you were going to keep it. This was an extension of the attitude I had already learned without knowing in Dayton.

Kihon Happo

The Japanese instructors were awe-inspiring. Noguchi Sensei himself was capable of physical athleticism which I know men in their 20s are completely incapable of. I remember one day he lay down flat on the floor and performed a form of press-up which involved putting his hands out above his head and moving his body into a half-moon position off the ground. I attempted to repeat this and found it impossible. Michael Pearce just laughed. It was a very valuable time for me. And every moment I had with one of these instructors was of great importance. I was always aware that there could be lessons that would pass me by. And one day, fate provided me with a magnificent gift.

I attended a class early in the morning with Hatsumi's oldest and longest-standing disciple, Oguri Sensei. I was the only person who had appeared for the class. The classes had been rather sparsely attended anyway, but on this day only I appeared, and we were both happy. Oguri embraced the opportunity. With a great smile, he said, "Kihon Happo. We do Kihon Happo." My Japanese isn't very good, but I knew that *Kihon* meant 'basic', and that *Happo* meant 'eight'. So this would translate as 'eight sets of basics exercises'. We were about to cover the basics.

Oguri explained that the Kihon Happo were the basic eight movements underlying the whole of martial arts, and that he was going to show them exactly as he had been taught them by Masaaki Hatsumi. Eight (八, *hachi*), he explained, is considered a lucky number in Japanese culture because the pictogram (八) broadens gradually, giving the idea of increasing prosperity.

The Japanese considered eight to be a holy number in ancient times. The reason for this is less well understood, but it is thought that it may be related to the fact they used eight to express the idea of large numbers vaguely such as manifold or infinity. Eight is also considered to be a holy number in Buddhism due to the Noble Eightfold Path.

It was wonderful to experience the eight basic techniques and how they could be applied not only in unarmed combat but also with weapons – and also to hear Oguri's thoughts on these techniques after a lifetime of practice.

The Bujinkan Kihon Happo

Koshi Kihon Sanpo Waza
The first three techniques are known as the *Koshi Sanpo Waza* (three striking method techniques). Each is named after a Kamae used in the technique. To feature all of the Kihon Happo would exceed the scope of this book but I have included photos of the first two techniques so the reader can get the feel of the exercises.
1. *Ichimonji Kihon no Kata*
The attacker punches to the head. The defender then drops diagonally backwards into Ichimonji to the right and performs an upper block to the

attacking arm. The defender then steps forward and performs a *Fudo Ken* to the head. *(See figs.48, 49, 50, 51)*

2. *Jumonji Kihon no Kata*

The attacker punches to the head. From *Jumonji no Kamae*, he blocks the punch, then performs a Boshi Ken to the armpit or ribs. *(See figs.52, 53, 54, 55)*

Fig.48

Fig.49

Fig.50

Fig.51

Here are descriptions for the rest of the set.

3. *Hicho Kihon no Kata*

The attacker kicks or punches to the stomach. The defender dodges by standing on one leg, as pictured. This Kamae is known as *Hicho* or 'flying bird stance'. While lifting the leg he simultaneously performs a low sweeping block and then kicks to the lower ribs. With one flowing movement he then drops forward and performs an Omote Shuto to the neck.

Torite Kihon Goho Kata

The next five techniques are known as the *Torite Goho* (five arm attacking methods).

Fig.52

Fig.53

Fig.54

Fig.55

4. *Omote Kote Gyaku Dori*

The attacker grabs the opponent's left lapel with the right hand and with his left punches to the head. The defender, from *Shizen no Kamae*, covers the attacker's hand with his left hand, placing his thumb into the back of their hand. He then falls back with his right leg to put the attacker off balance. He lowers his weight to lift the attacking hand off with a jerk, using both of his hands while applying a wrist lock.

5. *Omote Gyaku*

The attacker grabs the defender's lapel with his right hand. The defender covers this hand to prevent the attacker escaping/using it to punch. The defender steps diagonally back to the left, taking the attacker off balance, then performs an outer wrist lock. Stepping in close, the defender then locks the attacker's arm and takes him to the ground.

6. *Musha Dori*

The attacker makes a right forearm grab to his opponent's left arm. The defender brings his right arm up over and under the attacker's left arm to bend the elbow and apply a lock. He draws the attacker close to him with a sense of urgency. Keeping his right palm facing upwards, he places his two palms together and takes the opponent down with a kick to the back of the leg.

7. *Muso Dori*

The attacker grabs the defender's lapel with his right hand. The defender covers this hand with his left to prevent the attacker escaping/using it to punch. The defender steps forward and performs an elbow lock, taking the attacker to the ground.

8. *Ganseki Nage*

The attacker makes a left forearm grab with his right hand. The defender steps in, sending his left arm behind the attacker, clipping him on the back of his head, making sure he ends up very close to the attacker so as to be facing in the same direction. The left foot should be between the attacker's feet but slightly forward and facing in the same direction. The left shoulder should be under the attacker's right armpit and the left hip on the attacker's right hip. He rotates the body to the right without moving the legs to throw him across to the right and front.

Selfish Focus

Whenever I mentioned politics to Michael Pearce he answered in exactly the same way: "I don't care." If I talked to him about other people's problems and difficulties with the art, I got the same answer. He showed a complete disinterest in anything political or anything mundane happening around him. His focus was completely on his own training.

He explained to me one day, "You need to have your mind completely on Budō. You must have your mind on your own training. Even when you're teaching, you're there training for yourself. It's for the student to learn to be responsible for his own learning. You're just training with him. Always keep your focus on your own training. Never let it move to anything else. All this politics, this gossip, everything else around you, you have to ignore."

I noticed that this philosophy was one that was being practised by the Grand Master. Many times when I was there, during the latter part of my visit, westerners would come up with a question about something that someone was doing or what someone was up to. Hatsumi would either condemn or praise depending on what the person seemed to require at the moment. But he didn't care.

His love was martial arts. His love was the spirit of Ninjutsu. And this selfish focus was something that I found was somewhat of a requirement for continuing practice of the art. Our minds come up with so many alternatives to just doing what we're there to do. It's all very exciting, the soap opera of life, but it's not the purpose in our Ninja training.

My luck at being the only westerner in the Ninja classes ran out, and after two weeks of being tutored almost exclusively by the Japanese, floods of westerners appeared. Perhaps 'floods' is too much of an exaggeration, but in a very small dojo another three to five people makes a big difference. The bulk of this western invasion consisted of students from Australia, those whom I had met at my very first lesson.

Where they had been in the ensuing two weeks, I don't know. Probably travelling around Japan and experiencing the mountains. They were headed by a friendly giant of a man called Darren Howarth, and all of them seemed very positive and smiled almost continually.

They brought a very positive, pleasant feel to the dojo. Soon travellers from different countries around the world started to appear, as if they knew there was a receptive presence there for them. At this time, local peers began to move my training more outside the dojo.

We would attend Noguchi's personal dojo for lessons with him. Then Michael started taking more personal responsibility for my training, and it was far more one-on-one. Whether this was a response to the westerners' presence, I don't know, but it was good, as I started to see a little more of Japan.

Evading the Blade

In the evening, a lot of my training with Michael was what is termed 'Mutodori'. Mutodori means 'without the sword'. Every evening, over our beer and our squid legs, we would talk of martial arts and then, for up to an hour, I would be asked to dodge as Michael struck at me with a large club.

This club is a traditional Ninja weapon, and is basically a small tree trunk with a handle on the end. It's something that you only neglect to dodge once. Mutodori is extremely nerve-racking, tiring and intense, but it really did bring about a change in my awareness and reactions that no other training had done before.

This relentless dodging and fear of damage and attack started to give me a real vision of what it must have been like to be a feudal Ninja in Japan. But this club was not the only Ninja weapon. The whole Hombu dojo is an armoury of traditional weapons from various periods of Japanese history.

They have *Kusarigama Shogi*, which is a sickle with a chain and a loop on the end. Sometimes the Ninja would attach flaming objects to the end of the chain, or tie a venomous animal such as a snake or a scorpion to it, so that when the chain wrapped around the opponent he would be too busy dealing with the immediate flames or biting animal to avoid the sickle blade that would finish its task.

There were also a variety of swords and staffs of different lengths. There were knives, throwing weapons, whips, chains, every variety of spear, halberd, and other weapons very specific to the Ninja art, such as cat claws or small weapons for pressing pressure points. The list was endless.

But the weapon that I was taught to focus on at my stage of development was a small baton called a Hanbo. It was half the length of a normal bow staff, and about the same length as a police extendable baton. Many of the techniques practised by the police seem to have evolved from a traditional Hanbo school.

Crossfit

During my time in Japan, Michael Pearce put me on a training regime called Crossfit. It's a military-style training regime whereby each day a website updates what kind of physical exertion you are about to undertake. I found this extremely challenging, but I have managed to keep to the routine ever since. When you look in the mirror after the first six months you realise that you're physically fitter that you've ever been in your life.

Crossfit is based purely on functional exercise and is ideal for Ninja training because for climbing trees, keeping low stances or performing something dangerous in the dark you need to have adaptable physical skills to be able to run reasonable distances and to be able to lift weights, or at least lift your own body weight.

However, Crossfit started to take on a different angle for me after the first two months. My body was always aching. I never knew what I was going to be doing the next day, and there was only one day off per week. It started to take on a similar angle to the Yamabushi training I had undertaken having returned from Stephen Hayes. It was a hardship I had to learn to go through.

Until you practise this kind of level of physical exercise you can't begin to understand how much you come up against yourself. Many days you will find yourself feeling like you would rather do anything but exercise. But once you get yourself into the motion, everything starts to fall into place. Crossfit produced a toughness in my body and in my mind that nothing else has before, and it's something I intend to keep up, in one form or another, for the rest of my life.

Falconry

Michael Pearce took me to a restaurant one day where there was nothing but a shed on tarmac, but seemed to be the most popular restaurant in the whole of Japan. It was crowded to the brim with bustling people eager for their lunch. I ordered a curry, which I was told this restaurant was famous for.

When it appeared, I was surprised to see a plate almost literally overflowing with curry. This plate could have served a family of eight! There was more rice than I would cook for my whole family. The meat seemed to be some form of cutlet, possibly pork, covered in breadcrumbs but then smothered with a very thick curry sauce. And although the meal was delicious, I could barely eat a quarter. It was then time, said Michael, to go and learn about falconry.

Falconry was a good place to watch Shansin, with all this three-hearted warrior focus in action. It didn't disappoint. Both the falcon and the falconer experienced Shansin because you need to be completely in the moment.

Michael explained, "The three hearts can be seen in this situation: one heart is what you want, the second heart is what the falcon wants, and the third is what the Kami (Nature spirits) want. Which way is the wind going? Are you on a slope? What does the environment dictate? You have to control the falcon with treats – small bits of food. Don't ever give him too much or he'll no longer be hungry and you'll lose control. Keep the three hearts in mind in all things you do."

By now I knew how Michael worked. I knew this was a code. The three hearts he mentioned corresponded to the heaven, earth and man of the Ten Chi Jin. The lesson was also on two levels. My name Faulks also means 'falcon', and I knew that on one level I was the falcon being controlled with titbits.

The lesson was also in the practical act of falconry. Birds of prey have an amazing instinct and have such focus of the mind that we should all learn to imitate it and reproduce it in ourselves. However, the falconer has also to remain completely in the moment. One mistake could cause him a problem or injury. But it is not only birds of prey that bite.

Michael Pearce has viciousness in him. A viciousness and intensity that other instructors I've had did not possess. It's something that I believe he has gained from his direct long-term tuition from Masaaki Hatsumi. The Ninja of Noda are still genuine Ninja in every sense of the word.

And like the man who sought out the most rare venomous snake and then died from being bitten by it, if you seek to interact with them you should be careful, and be aware that these are genuine warriors, not pretend wannabes or movie star wish fulfilments.

Dealing with Danger!

One day I was talking to a few of the western students about my training and was taken to one side. It was explained to me that Stephen Hayes had been very disrespectful to the Grand Master and that I should not mention his name. I was also told that his black belt had been taken down from the dojo and that the members of the dojo had been told that if they trained with Stephen Hayes they were to break him. They then asked me many questions as to when I last saw Stephen and regarding his health.

I was in shock. Suddenly everything made sense. That was why James Norris was sent to meet me first, as a scouting party to see if everything was OK. This was why Hayes was so evasive, careful and unpredictable. I knew that Hayes and Hatsumi were still in touch and that he had not been expelled from the organisation, but I also knew that Stephen had renamed his art and gone it alone. Stephen said that he had done this due to the terrible standards and misunderstandings of the art in the west.

The students in Japan claimed that Stephen had not been able to cope with a change in the ranking system that added an increased number of Dans to the black belt grades from 12 to 15.

If they had known Stephen as I did, they would have realised that he was moved by abstracts, so it would have had to be something bigger than that – something about the direction in himself or in the Bujinkan. Whatever the truth, I was quite sure that Master Hatsumi barely gave it a second thought. His focus was always on Budō and the higher teachings. Then something unexpected happened. They threatened me.

"Where do you live in England?"

I told them.

"We can have someone at your door in 30 minutes if you betray us."

I was taken aback. That seemed a very strange approach. What did they expect me to do? Why go directly to such a statement?

However, when I thought about it, I realised I had been naive. Did I really think that Japan's most legendary assassins would be gentle and wear flowers in their hair? Did I think I was in a film? I had travelled into a cave to find a rare and deadly snake in order to learn from observing its movements; then having found it, I was shocked that it hissed at me.

Then it hit me like a thunderbolt. Something that no one else could see. They had no idea what they were dealing with. Hatsumi Sensei. He was more a Ninja than any of us. Ninjutsu at its base level is the art of making people do what you want; perhaps an even better description would be the art of making what you want happen. Why couldn't they see it was all part of his great plan? He was still the teacher of Stephen Hayes. If he had wanted to, did they not think that the world's greatest Ninja would be able to control a disrespectful student? His strategy and cunning were far beyond anything we could even think of! Compared to him, we were children. If something in his environment had happened it was because he had either made it happen or had allowed it to happen, something that someone who had never experienced the power of Ninja strategy before could never understand.

He had made all this happen. The danger, the rejection from the Bujinkan society, all of this was part of making Stephen the Ninja he was now. Living with constant threat and having to make it on his own.

It was at this moment I realised that my wife had been right. Ninjutsu is not something everyone can fully grasp. As humans we tend to be unfocused and undirected; we tend to look on the surface of things and accept them without thinking.

But Ninjutsu is about duplicity.

Duplicity

I observed life at the Hombu dojo. I observed people's interaction with each other. I had used a completely different strategy then from the approach I had used in America. I came to Japan quiet, trying to fit in, and being cautious rather than loud, boastful and aggressive. Because of this, I saw a lot more than perhaps most visitors would. I started to become invisible in the dojo. I was always there far too early for class, and always left late.

I noticed something amazing about Masaaki Hatsumi. He was able to give completely different personas to different people. And indeed, the answers he would give to questions would also differ depending on the person. In a strange way, it seemed as if he was telling people to follow their heart.

If someone came to him asking if meditation was important, he would reassure them that it was. If someone came to him asking whether he agreed that meditation wasn't important, he would say, "Why no, of course; we're martial artists, not Buddhist monks." He seemed to be able to adapt, and had a duplicity that made him the perfect instructor for everyone. It was like they were talking to the mirror.

Now one side of this which is worth mentioning is that it caused arguments amongst different senior figures within the Ninja world. If a very spiritual person was under the tuition of Hatsumi, he would ask spiritual questions and gain answers that others would not. If a very dedicated warrior and martial artist were to talk to Hatsumi, Hatsumi would focus on warrior disciplines and on the importance of physical technique. Everyone around him was a whirl of emotions and drama, whereas Hatsumi was still in the middle and focused on Budō. Now I understood the reason for Michael Pearce's selfish focus on the art.

This flexibility has led to a great variety of approaches and thoughts about Ninjutsu. But very few people seem to have noticed how this has come about. Each instructor is utterly convinced beyond compare that his approach is absolutely correct and mistrusts the conflicting or different teachings of other instructors. All claim, of course, to have been taught these specific techniques by their master, when in fact what they have been taught is to be themselves – to find the route to power that works for them, and to become their own Ninja master.

Masaaki Hatsumi says in one of his books that he had written to the Ninja ancestors of Mount Togakure asking for the true secrets of Ninjutsu and 40 years later he had been sent a reply. When he opened the envelope, it contained a blank piece of paper.

In Japan, I discovered that Ninjutsu is whatever works. Whatever is in your heart and whoever you are.

The Blank Paper

When I reflect on my Ninjutsu training it seems to have been guided by fate. My first teacher was a thief, a man of the underworld, an assassin. He taught me skills they no longer teach in Japan and I benefited from his years of dedication to this side of the art. Karl had a rough form of enlightenment that came with a sense of resentment about the world. I can't explain how, but something about this resentful view opens you up to being creative and resourceful.

Next came Stephen Hayes, the mystic; a man who had dedicated his entire life to enlightenment and esoteric studies. Here I gained a training in both meditative and active mind control techniques. His tuition broadened my world view in every sense of the word.

Finally came my tuition in Japan, where the former teachings are not taught and the path is that of the warriors – Budō. For them it is all about the perfection of combat skills.

It occurs to me that a Ninja is all three of the above – a thief, a mystic and a warrior – and that fate, by guiding me to each teacher in turn, has left me with the complete range of Ninja skills. It has also given me a choice of areas to specialise in. I am convinced that all three are routes to the same outcome. The thief gains enlightenment and combat skills from his art if he does it correctly. The mystic gains abilities of combat and stealth through his understanding. The warrior turns his battle spiritually inside. Perhaps this could be seen as Shansin or the three hearts Hatsumi spoke of.

What I do know is that I am beginning to understand that the Ninja path is not set or rigid, but is something you need to find for yourself. You cannot rely on any teacher or any manual to reveal the truth to you.

The Shinto Shrine
It was my last day in Noda city. After a month of training with the greatest martial artists the world has to offer, I was about to return to my wife and family in England.

I felt sadness, but also relief. Physically, my body had started to adapt. It felt that just as I was starting to get into the flow of life in Noda it was time to leave. It had been the most monumentally challenging time of my entire life.

Japan was so different in every way. Ninjutsu was not a path for the faint-hearted. As I wandered back towards my ryokan after my final evening with Michael Pearce, I decided to visit the Shinto shrine in Noda one last time. As I stood facing the altar, I clapped, bowed, clapped again, and made an offering of 30 yen to the Kami.

I prayed to them that as I returned to England, I would take the true secrets and true understanding of the Ninja path with me, that I would continue along the correct direction with my training, and that good would be the result. And then something spectacular happened; something I wouldn't have believed if I hadn't been there myself. As soon as the coin hit the bottom of the altar chest, there was a strike of lightning across the sky and a giant rumble of thunder and torrential rain came down upon Noda. The Kami evidently were listening, which I interpreted as a very good sign.

As I walked through the rain, I didn't worry about getting wet. I knew that, somehow, some of the spirits of Mount Togakure had become part of me, and would always be part of me, no matter where I went.

Gaining a Black Belt
I had a cold and early start on the morning of my flight back to Britain. I knew I would have to be catching trains and getting through the hustle and bustle of Tokyo, which would be a stark contrast to what I had become used to in the peaceful world of Noda.

As I said my goodbyes and changed out of my slippers in order to put my outdoor shoes on, Michael Pearce appeared. It was very early for Michael to be up and he had something with him.

"This is for you." He handed me a plastic bag. I opened it and inside was a beautiful ornate black belt. The symbolism behind this gift was more than the object itself. Inside was a certificate which bore the signature and mark of Masaaki Hatsumi and the names of the nine stories in Ninjutsu listed in Japanese.

"I'm very emotional and very proud," said Michael. This came as a shock as well. During the whole trip he had been extremely critical of my technique, continually correcting me and often reminding me how far I had got to go. This was the first praise I had ever heard from him.

"You've worked real hard and you've learned the most important lesson."

I looked at him and I knew what he meant. I had learned how to be a student, learned how to practise the art. Just like the curry, when I ordered my bowl of Ninjutsu it had been more than I could possibly cope with. But now I had learned that, little and often and gently working away daily, just like growing the Bonsai, the Ninjutsu was an ongoing task. And I must continue working at it for the rest of my life.

A black belt in Togakure Budō Taijutsu, the unarmed combat of a Ninja, was an achievement I never thought I would reach. Ninja is such a high-level art that it's very hard to get even the first foundations of attainment. Many people give up or decide on taking an easier way. As I boarded my train I realised that I, too, was proud of what I had achieved. But this black belt didn't signify mastery; it signified a beginning.

CHAPTER SEVEN

THE RETURN FROM JAPAN

A s I sat on the train, ready to catch another train, to catch my flight, in turn to catch other trains, and then to drive back home, the true meaning of the Shi-kin hara-mitsu dai-ko-myo came to me.

The Ninja interprets everything in life as part of his training, for he has been a Ninja since birth. We are all following the way of enduring and overcoming. Every event that happens in life is something we should learn from, and I had found a way of making this happen, whether it had been bad or whether it had been good.

Ninjutsu is about continuing on, no matter what. And as I returned to England I could see in front of me a great challenge. I had a terrible sense of divided loyalty. I felt a great loyalty for both parties – parties at war. Because of their differences, I had gained more than I could ever gain by training with one school. Their questioning of each other helped me decide what was of value to me. The truth was that each layer of teaching had had such value that I couldn't bear the idea of discounting or rejecting any of it.

In America I had found people who I related to and who had really cared for me. I had learned skills which I felt were valuable beyond words from Stephen Hayes, and I had bonded with the community at Dayton. Learning at the To-Shin Do school, you are part of a team: your teacher is as excited about your progress as you are.

Not so in Japan. Learning in Japan is learning the hard way. They just feed the students a martial arts class. Most people don't want any more and thus don't see any more. If you really wanted to get the whole art you would have to contemplate deeply everything said by a teacher and take full personal responsibility for your learning. I suspect the whole thing has been set up deliberately like this to ensure that only those who are absolutely willing to fight for the art get the true teachings. The teachers are really focused on their Budō. To learn the whole art of Ninjutsu you would have to go in with everything you had and steal the art. If anyone says you can no longer learn genuine Ninjutsu in Japan, they are wrong. But you are going to have to fight for it every step of the way. Otherwise you will simply learn self-defence, nothing more. Fight for every lesson and continually question. I suspect this is why the lessons are so strange outside Japan because few people can even grasp this art.

I was lucky I had found Michael Pearce, Noguchi Sensei and instructors who made the experience extremely valuable to me. Without them, I wouldn't have gained any of the specialist knowledge and understanding. I would have simply been a man attending martial art classes. In fact I believe that the vast majority of people visiting Japan get from their stay but a small fraction of what I did, without the fortunate guidance I received. I think this is why the classes are so strange in US and British dojos.

I decided I would have to ignore all politics and honestly pursue the art. That, after all, is what Hatsumi did! I realised that I was being held back by fear of criticism from others and that I had to focus on effectiveness of my methods whether the Ninja world approved or not. I would continue my Ninja training and gravitate to whoever and wherever I could most efficiently learn the real and effective art.

The Way of Truth

The real changes to my life and being began to happen in the months after my Japanese adventure. Ninjutsu was changing for me. As my ability to understand things started to open up, so my strategic thinking improved. The world began to change. I can't quite describe it, but moments of revelation as to the true motives of my actions and those of others appeared to me regularly. It was like an illusion was slowly being washed away. People around me seemed asleep and unaware. They floated through life, only able to hold on to an aim for a few moments before their emotions redirected them as they became distracted. It was as though they couldn't see beyond the surface of things.

I started to realise that I had been the same. I began to appreciate how being a Ninja was about being able to make something inside endure, to keep focused on your true goal. Knowing your purpose in life and living for that purpose, just as the Ninja keeps focused on his mission and does not let emotions, distractions or hardships get in the way. In Japan they call this *Fudōshin* (immovable heart): a state of equanimity or imperturbability. Being honest with yourself and being sure of your true intentions is a skill. As you get better at it, the more powerful and focused you become.

But as this process of peeling away the illusion continued, things started to change in other ways.

Beat – It's Like Outliving Jazz

Kitty la Roar! My friend and I both laughed; we were delighted at the humour in the name.

"The guy on the piano's called Nick of Time," said the doorman without humour. As we entered the jazz club various people in our group started to rebel. It was small, cramped and smelly. The music, however, was transfixing and I was hooked. As the evening continued I was deserted by each of my friends, one by one. I just sat there, enjoying the show. It was like a trip in the past. The elegant Kitty held the room with her voice.

I had never really been a fan of jazz music, but I knew for my Ninja training that to pick up the feel of the art I would have to go and see someone performing and be with them as they practised their art.

The phrase uttered by Hatsumi had echoed in my mind. It had puzzled me, I couldn't let go of it, just kept mulling it over in my mind. I had examined it from so many different angles, but nothing ever really clicked. I decided that if I was to learn the true meaning of this phrase I needed to know more about jazz itself. If I had learned anything from my training, it was that you had to learn from doing.

That evening was the start of a friendship with both Kitty and Nick, our differences being the most powerful thing. Whenever I was in London I went to see them and after the gigs Kitty and I would talk. We became the best of friends. The nature of the friendship continually pushed us both out of our comfort zones. I had been brought up in a very disciplined way; I had started my martial arts training at the age of 5. At the time of writing it has been 18 years since I missed a day of meditation and martial training. My life is and always has been planned, routine and disciplined. I had never really spent time going out in my teens and didn't really party. My life was full of great quests and aims; I didn't do many things just for the sake of fun.

Kitty was continually trying to get me to do things I was not comfortable with – singing, dancing and generally partying. Her world view was very different from mine. To me, life is a great mission; to her it's a celebration! In Kitty's world and those around her, very little seemed to be planned; everything was responsive to the situation at hand. She, in turn, was having evenings filled with conversations on Taoism and acupuncture, and receiving instructions on meditation through the post! It was an wonderful exchange; I was learning about creativity and improvisation and she was learning the way of strategy and spirituality.

It was through this dynamic friendship that it suddenly hit me, not merely in an intellectual sense but also on a deep emotional level, and I started to understand the hidden message. Just by association I started to pick up Kitty's responsive creativity. Kitty was very clever and reacted and adapted to the world like in improvisational jazz.

I suddenly realised the meaning behind what Hatsumi had said. When he said "It's like outliving jazz" he was trying to explain how Ninja combat strategy is about an emotive, responsive, creative and adaptive response to the flow and beat of the events around you. An emotive flow response to a pattern. With my new level of emotion and sudden outburst in creativity I started to be able to see opportunities I never had. I would become inspired like an artist or musician and the whole master plan would flow. It was something I had never felt before, something strong and powerful inside. This was the final lesson I needed to complete my strategic training. Suddenly I had it. Even when I was in combat, with the beat of the opponent's attacks I could feel the music and know when to counter. Something would hit me with a sudden burst of artistic inspiration and it was just like the feeling of fire inside. I instantly knew how I would bring about the destruction of my enemy. I listened to the song 'Temptation' by Heaven 17 that Hatsumi had mentioned and suddenly I knew what he had meant.

Don't get me wrong. This is not the answer to strategic or martial power. It's the element at the end. Alone it is quite weak, like having a can of petrol but no car. You can cause a lot of light and heat but can't go anywhere. But combining the elements, the Ten Chi Jin, the ability to recognise the musical pattern behind events and being inspired by the flow is the key to amazing power. I began to achieve incredible success in everything I did. Six months after my time in Japan, a phrase used in the class with Hatsumi Sensei suddenly made sense.

Strategy and Power

With my new strategic abilities I found myself able to achieve far more than I had ever before been able to do in my life. I was more successful at work and gained promotion. I started to be able to make a lot more money both for my employer and in my spare time effortlessly. I began to test myself and found I could think of solutions or ways of achieving almost anything. I was no longer restricted by myself. If I set my mind on achieving something, I could just do it. If I wanted to meet someone – whether it be a member of the Royal Family or a film star – I would simply find a way to go and meet them. If I wanted to travel somewhere, I would do so. I started to set myself increasingly outlandish and extravagant goals. I was searching for my limitations; something I was beginning to find hard to achieve.

Emotions and the Importance of Things

I started to realise how people around me were unaware of how precious every moment of life is. It was as though they didn't realise what was going on. Inside me a great emotion grew: an urge to save them from this daydream. All about me I saw people with dreams and goals in life, people whose every action would cause them to fail. I could see couples living together with completely different goals, neither of them realising how one of them would go to their deathbed with their dreams shattered, and both unwilling to face the conflict. Everything began to seem like a tragedy to me. So many people born with dreams and going to their graves without the slightest realisation of them. I was filled with the most tremendous feelings of love and compassion and the most terrible feelings of mourning and sadness. I started helping my friends and people I met in my spare time. With my new skills I could see ways of making things happen in a way that others couldn't. As this continued, I found myself gradually getting tired and hurt. It seemed that many people didn't really want their dreams to come true. Often when presented with their dream, they would reject it or subconsciously sabotage things. Sometimes anger would be the result. The urge to be a hero that had first started my quest had now become a terrible debilitating weakness. I was losing my own strength and expending my power on every crying female or lame duck I met. I had to take a hold of myself and start focusing on those who really wanted help, people who were willing to fight for their goals or were in grave danger. It was difficult, as I realised that I had been gaining a lot from these quests and it pained me to let go of this behaviour. But I had to focus on the big picture and put my skills to the best use.

Replacing Karl and Shaun

With Shaun in the Philippines and Karl travelling around the world as a gun for hire, I was left in their area. The legend had continued. By now I had inherited all their equipment and started taking on a role similar to theirs in the past, but with this important difference: I used the easiest route. Most times when someone is in trouble it is easiest to simply gather evidence and present it to the police – something Karl and Shaun would never consider doing. Even if the evidence is not usable in court, once the police officers know who the problem is, they will focus and find a way of dealing with it. In fact as I have gained in experience I have found that rather than spending huge amounts of time trying to turn life into a nightmare, it is far better to focus that energy on making your life into a dream. Only the most persistent of enemies has to be dealt with. The truth is that most of our problems in life are of our own making and they can be solved by working out why we keep causing them to happen.

A Return to Nature
Isolated in England with no kindred spirit nearby, I focused on learning from my greatest teachers – Nature and life. I practised my Taijutsu in the dark every night. I focused on making my movement relaxed, flowing and natural. I continued to test myself against the elements with Yamabushi training and to challenge Nature as Karl and Shaun had done, by attempting to travel silently through all terrain and to approach animals and people without being detected. During my daily life I watched how the elements tested me and fought to overcome them and keep my equilibrium at all costs. It is the duty of a Ninja with all the power he has at his disposal to keep his inner calm and equilibrium.

Everything started to flow together. The movements I made without weapons and those with weapons become the same; my climbing, running, weightlifting and even my lock picking started to cross-pollinate. An improvement or insight in one skill would suddenly lead to a similar improvement in another. I began to develop an inner resilience I had never felt before. I started to lose many of the feelings that had held me back in the past. The challenge was now between me and Nature; the opinions and thoughts of other people lost all relevance or importance. Nature had become my guide. I was no longer practising Ninjutsu, I was a Ninja. The art was in everything I did.

Continually Challenging Yourself
On my return I just couldn't settle into any class. None of them matched up. I suppose they had a hard act to follow and, besides, my Ninjutsu was not many other people's Ninjutsu. To me it is about challenging yourself and pushing the boundaries, about overcoming your limitations and realising your hidden potential. The world of Ninja training has become stiff and limited like karate or any other martial art. I wanted to do something to raise its game, to bring respect and awe back to our art. To do this I started to make my challenges public, something I knew only Stephen Hayes to have done in the past.

I discovered that the greatest power I had was in my faults. I have always been a playful and obsessive person, so I learned to channel these two qualities like never before. I would give myself spectacular challenges and then do everything to achieve them. Through this approach my abilities began to progress far beyond anything before and I would often video myself and play it back. When the video was ready I would present it to the world. Through this method I learned acrobatics and amazingly accurate Shuriken throwing. I learned to climb trees using cat claws faster than anyone I had ever seen. Soon I decided it was time for a very public display of what I felt was the greatest Ninja skill.

The Stealthiest Man Alive?

An American-based documentary company called Reality Entertainment approached me to demonstrate my Ninja skills for transmission on Sky TV and several American cable channels. The whole thing was about stealth, which is the area of my Ninja training that, thanks to Karl, I have the greatest confidence in. Stealth is a complicated art with many aspects to it. It's not just about how silent you are, it's also about how visible you are, and how much you fit in with the environment. It's no use being totally silent if you are in plain view. This challenge, however, was focused completely on sound, and it was a challenge no one had ever attempted before.

In front of the world I was asked to prove that with my years of Ninja training I was more silent than any other living predator! Using the most sophisticated scientific equipment, the staff at Dartmoor Zoological Park were going to trigger the stealth response in a wolf, a tiger, a lion, and – the biggest challenge – in the most silent of big cats: a jaguar.

This is what zoologists have to say about the jaguar.

"The cat will walk slowly down forest paths, listening for and stalking prey before rushing or ambushing. The jaguar attacks from cover and usually from a target's blind spot with a quick pounce; the species' stealth abilities are considered nearly peerless in the animal kingdom by both indigenous people and field researchers, and are probably a product of its role as an apex predator in several different environments."

The sound levels of each animal were to be recorded and I would then be challenged to cross the same area of land in an attempt to outdo Nature. It was a big challenge!

How could I win? The jaguar has many advantages: it walks on all fours, it's a born predator and has paws made for stealth. I was going to use my mind and Ninjutsu to overcome the animal's innate abilities. The truth was that the documentary makers had made some bad choices of opponent. The wolf and lion were not really much of a challenge as neither of them relies on stealth, using pack behaviour and speed to their advantage. The tiger and jaguar, however, were a different matter.

The first time we were booked for the challenge it was rained off. There were gale force winds and the zoo had to put the animals away, for if a tree fell it could cause them to escape. This gave me a great advantage as I was able to experiment with the recording equipment and find which noises did and didn't stand out against background noise. I also got to see the environment that I would be challenged in, and this formulated my master plan. I decided I would move in time with the background noise or when the recording equipment was moved or knocked. The animals, of course, would not.

The day of the challenge came. It was a cold day and everyone was shivering. As they tested each and every animal in turn, I did my best to cause problems for my unknowing rivals. I insisted that the challenge took place on the same piece of land. This meant that the animals had to be moved around, which upset them. I made sure that with each challenge, the scent of the previous animal and the bait from the previous challenge were there to confuse them. Most of all, I made sure that the jaguar took the challenge after being fed, so he was far less motivated. I watched the sound ratings on the screen as they came in. The wolf and lion, as I suspected, were the worst. The tiger made only a small amount of noise, and the jaguar was virtually silent. The only way I was going to win this was to be *totally* silent, to make no noise in any way!

I took 10 minutes to meditate and bring about a total sense of calmness. I indicated to the crew I was about to start and took a deep breath. One single twig or loose stone and I would be a laughing stock in front of the world, and I would have let down every teacher I had ever had. I had watched the route of the jaguar during his test. After all, he would know the best route in his own territory. However, I was surprised to see that he took a direct route to his prey over grass and muddy areas. I decided to ignore his judgement and to take a route alongside the fence where there was a rim of concrete all the way along. This, I thought, would be the easy option.

The challenge was about noise, so I did not worry about my visibility and focused all my energy on being silent. I was slow, very slow, and moved only when a car passed, someone coughed or when the staff holding the microphone lost concentration. I took advantage of every distraction, background noise, wolf's howl or lion's roar. I was patient and gentle, but it was terribly stressful not knowing at any one point how I was doing or if I had failed. But then it hit. Suddenly my body was on fire. Pain ran through every fibre of my being. I squatted down instinctively and the pain stopped as I moved. It took me a few moments to realise: the fence was electrified and I had just made full contact. No wonder the jaguar had avoided it. It was a wonder I had not been shocked the moment I started, as you didn't even have to touch the fence for the electricity to jump to your body and give you a shock.

Now I had to finish the test without changing route, with the dual focus of keeping silent and not getting too near the fence. The tension was horrible. By the end of the test I was exhausted and soaked with sweat.

As I started to unpeel my Ninja uniform, the director Phil Gardiner approached me.

"Congratulations, you're as stealthy as a jaguar!"

I almost fainted. Although I had not beaten the jaguar, I was definitely in the same league. I had matched the best nature had to offer and proven the genuineness of my art.

Finding the True Self – Letting Go of Your Limitations

The culmination of this process hit me one day. I was performing meditation in some woods and suddenly the lightning bolt struck. Just as my perceptions of how things worked and how to do things had held me back in the past, so too had the perceptions of who I am. Perhaps to be the total master of your own mind you simply had to believe yourself to be so.

I once heard that when the Ninja first appeared in Japan they shocked the world by attacking and escaping through the walls of the houses. In those times, the walls were made of paper, but because of the perception of them being solid, people had never attacked through them, and if chased into a room with no way out had given themselves up or been killed my their captors. The Ninja with his new ability to see things in a different way had shocked the world by simply jumping through the wall. I have found that almost all our limitations are like these paper walls; we can simply break through them if we realise that they are not real limitations but simply things put in place to make borders for our own comfort.

Perhaps we all hold ourselves back from achieving our true potential because we are not willing to take responsibility for our actions and our power. We hold on to our faults and our weaknesses because we enjoy them. They give us drama and in a way we are addicted to them. If we let go of them we would have to take responsibility for everything.

All the tools we have evolved to improve ourselves are really just here to help us gain confidence and come to terms with our inherent power. We are all enlightened and the masters of our own minds; it is just accepting that state that we struggle with. Leading from this insight I found that if I acted the part of the person I always dreamed of being, that reality started to rapidly shift in that direction.

Now as I stood at the perimeter of the airfield that had obsessed Karl and Shaun, I understood. Once I had been reduced to a state of terror, scared by the possibility of failure. The guards had special training, strong defences and far superior weapons. As I looked out past the barbed-wire fence I felt no fear. I had something far more powerful... I had Ninjutsu.

USEFUL CONTACTS

Martin Faulks
Visit my website to keep up with my Ninja Adventures.
www.martinfaulks.com

Stephen K. Hayes – *To-Shin Do*
If you want to train in To-Shin Do I suggest you visit this website to find your local class. Or why not book some private lessons with Stephen K. Hayes and learn from one of the greatest living martial artists?
http://www.skhquest.com

Michael Pearce
Would you like to travel to Noda in Japan to train with Grand Master Masaaki Hatsumi? Contact Michael if you are serious about walking the Ninja path.
http://web.me.com/mpearce/Training_and_travel/Welcome.html

Crossfit
Crossfit is a strength and conditioning fitness methodology. Its stated goal is to create "the quintessential athlete, equal parts gymnast, Olympic weightlifter and sprinter. Crossfit is not sport-specific and promotes broad and general overall physical fitness."
Crossfit doubled my lifting ability and took my arm measurement from 13 inches to 15½.
http://www.crossfit.com

Spy Gadgets
Want spy gadgets like those described in this book? This is the best site.
http://www.spyonyou.co.uk